G. K. Chesterton's Early Poetry

Books from Inkling

Chesterton Day by Day by G. K. Chesterton. Daily readings from the writings of Chesterton selected by their author. (Includes notes on the context.)
ISBN: 1-58742-014-7 (paperback) & 1-58742-015-5 (hardback)

Eugenics and Other Evils by G. K. Chesterton. In the early twentieth century eugenics was considered enlightened, scientific, and progressive. Chesterton wrote one of the few book-length criticisms of eugenics published during that era.
ISBN: 1-58742-002-3 (paperback) & 1-58742-006-6 (hardback)

Celebrating Middle-earth edited by John West. Six Tolkien scholars (including Peter Kreeft and Joseph Pearce) comment on the literary, political and religious ideas in J. R. R. Tolkien's *The Lord of the Rings*.
ISBN: 1-58742-012-0 (paperback) & 1-58742-013-9 (hardback)

Untangling Tolkien by Michael W. Perry. Tolkien spent untold hours getting the dates in his tale right. This is the first detailed, book-length chronology for *The Lord of the Rings*. (Polish translation: *Klucz Do Tolkiena.*)
ISBN: 1-58742-019-8 (paperback)

Theism and Humanism by Arthur J. Balfour. C. S. Lewis praised this book as one of the ten books that most influenced his thought.
ISBN: 1-58742-005-8 (paperback) & 1-58742-016-3 (hardback)

On the Lines of Morris' Romances by William Morris. In a 1914 letter to his future wife, J. R. R. Tolkien described the beginning of his great tales about Middle-earth, when he told her he was writing "a short story somewhat on the lines of Morris' romances." Here under one cover are Morris' two great quest romances, *The Wood Beyond the World* and *The Well at the World's End*. Both are also available separately.
ISBN: *On the Lines of Morris' Romances*: 1-58742-024-4 (paperback)
The Wood Beyond the World: 1-58742-029-5 (paperback) & 1-58742-030-9 (hardback)
The Well at the World's End: 1-58742-31-7 (paperback) & 1-58742-032-5 (hardback)

More to William Morris by William Morris. In a 1960 letter, J. R. R. Tolkien wrote that parts of *The Lord of the Rings* "owe more to William Morris and his Huns and Romans, as in *The House of the Wolfings* or *The Roots of the Mountains*." Here under one cover are those two classic tales of courage and romance set in long-ago times. Both are also available separately.
ISBN: *More to William Morris*: 1-58742-023-6 (paperback).
The House of the Wolfings: 1-58742-025-2 (paperback) & 1-58742-026-0 (hardback).
The Roots of the Mountains: 1-58742-027-9 (paperback) & 1-58742-28-7 (hardback)

Bookstores can order these books from Baker & Taylor or Ingram (U.S.) or Bertrams (Europe). Also available online internationally.

G. K. Chesterton's Early Poetry

Greybeards at Play
The Wild Knight and Other Poems
The Ballad of the White Horse

by

G. K. Chesterton

Introductions by Michael W. Perry

Inkling Books   Seattle   2004

Description

This newly typeset book contains the full text and illustrations of G. K. Chesterton's first three books of poetry—*Greybeards at Play*, *The White Knight and Other Poems*, and *The Ballad of the White Horse*—in one edition intended for general readers. The first editions of the first two books listed the author as "Gilbert Chesterton."

Publisher's Note

Greybeards at Play (October 1900) was Chesterton's first book. This text is based on the first edition, which was published in London by R. Brimley Johnson. It contains all the original text and illustrations. "E.C.B." is Edmund Clerihew Bentley, a friend.

The Wild Knight and Other Poems was published in November 1900. This text is based on the first edition published in London by Grant Richards. It differs from the original in only one respect. In that edition, an additional poem, "Good News," was added at the end (after "The Wild Knight") but not listed in the "Contents." The poem is now the last before "The Wild Knight." That edition contained this "Note" from the author: "My thanks are due to the Editors of the *Outlook* and the *Speaker* for the kind permission they have given me to reprint a considerable number of the following poems. They have been selected and arranged rather with a view to unity of spirit than to unity of time or value; many of them being juvenile."

The Ballad of the White Horse (August 1911) was Chesterton's third book of poetry and was dedicated "To my wife." This text follows the UK first edition, but includes minor corrections made for *The Collected Poems of G. K. Chesterton* (1931). See Bk. 1, 180–183; Bk. IV, 9; and Bk. VI, 17. The 1911 U.S. edition punctuation is different.

The titles and headings use Adobe Caslon Pro, based on an eighteenth-century design by William Caslon. The text uses Adobe Jenson Pro, based on Renaissance typefaces.

Library Cataloging Data

G. K. Chesterton's Early Poetry: Greybeards at Play, The White Knight and Other Poems, The Ballad of the White Horse

G. K. Chesterton (1874–1936) with two introductions by Michael W. Perry (1948–)

231 pages, 6 x 9 x 0.5 inches, 229 x 152 mm. 26 illustrations (24 by Chesterton)

Library of Congress Control Number: 2004109135

ISBN: 1-58742-034-1 (alkaline paperback) 1-58742-035-X (alkaline hardback)

Publisher Information

First Inkling Books edition, First Printing, September 2004. Published in the United States of America on acid-free paper. Inkling Books, Seattle, WA, U.S.A. Internet: http://www.InklingBooks.com/

Contents

GREYBEARDS AT PLAY

Literature and Art
For Old Gentlemen

Rhymes and Sketches

by

G. K. CHESTERTON

Introduction:
Greybeards at Play and
The Wild Knight and Other Poems

The first two books in this collection began with a family tragedy. Chesterton was in love with Francis Blogg in the spring of 1899, when her sister Gertrude died after being hit by a bus. Francis became depressed and all his efforts to cheer her up failed, so he decided that the only way to save her from the darkness into which she was descending was for the two to marry. Unfortunately, his writing as yet earned little and the reading he did for a publisher, Fisher-Unwin, paid only a pittance.

Chesterton turned to his father for help. His father tried to negotiate a raise, but found Fisher-Unwin would only pay more if Chesterton worked more. That would make it harder for him to succeed as a writer. His father concluded that his son needed a successful book.

Two books resulted, with *Greybeards at Play* coming out in October of 1900, one month before *The Wild Knight and Other Poems*. Readers who are having trouble breaking into print should take heart from Chesterton. The first, as Alzina Dale notes in *The Outline of Sanity*, "was close to vanity publishing, because it was put out by Gertrude's former fiancé, Brimley Johnson." The second had so much trouble finding a publisher, that Chesterton's father ended up paying for its release. Despite its marvelously playful humor, *Greybeards* has passed into oblivion almost unnoticed, and Chesterton himself rarely mentioned it afterward. *Wild Knight* did a little better, but it was Chesterton's undeniable skill as a journalist that provided him with the money to marry. (His first newspaper writing was published in 1901 as *The Defendant.*)

As the reader will discover, *Greybeards at Play* deserves far more attention than it has thus far received. In his contribution to *G. K. Chesterton: A Centenary Appraisal*, the poet W. H. Auden noted:

> I have no hesitation in saying that it contains some of the best pure nonsense verse in English.... Surely, it is high time such enchanting pieces should be made readily available.... By natural gift, Chesterton was, I think, essentially a comic poet. Very few of his 'serious' poems are as good as these.

Of course, Chesterton's *The Wild Knight and Other Stories* has poems every bit as good at those in *Greybeards*, particularly the often quoted "By the Babe Unborn" and "The Donkey." But what are we to make of the book's strange central poem, "The Wild Knight"?

Christopher Hollis gives us a clue in *The Mind of Chesterton*. The story seems rooted in an experience Chesterton had while studying art at The Slade School. Standing on a long stairway, he had a heated debate with another student. Chesterton claimed, as Hollis put it, that "to seduce a virgin was as if one were to quench a star. Things had their nature, and virtue consisted of respecting that nature." His foe argued that "the object of life was to collect as many experiences as possible," and when natural experiences were exhausted, you turned to the unnatural and cruel. He added, "What you call evil, I call good."

But the story did not end there. Later Chesterton overhead his opponent say, "If I do that, I shan't know the difference between right and wrong." Chesterton never learned what sort of evil would make such an evil man shudder. But out of that experience he learned, "that there was indeed evil in the world but that even great evil could not quite escape the tug toward goodness."

Understand that and you grasp what is perhaps the underlying message of "The Wild Knight." In that tale, Lord Orm is so given over to evil that he has tried to seduce the beautiful Lady Olive. To protect her, Captain Redfeather intends to force Lord Orm into a fight, believing that even the evil serve "one last law. When I say 'Coward,' is the law awake." That is the "tug toward goodness."

But the captain discovers that Lord Orm is not even bound by that law. He seems to have "broken the last bond of man," becoming "perfectly free and utterly alone." As the reader will discover, it is the Wild Knight in his madness who stumbles across the "one last law" that Lord Orm will obey, and the secret he will kill to conceal.

I will introduce Chesterton's great epic poem, *The Ballad of the White Horse*, later in this book. For now, I leave you to the playful delights of Chesterton's great comic masterpiece, *Greybeards at Play*.

Michael W. Perry, Seattle, September 11, 2004

A Dedication

To E. C. B.

He was, through boyhood's storm and shower,
My best, my nearest friend;
We wore one hat, smoked one cigar,
One standing at each end.

We were two hearts with single hope,   5
Two faces in one hood;
I knew the secrets of his youth;
I watched his every mood.

The little things that none but I   9
Saw were beyond his wont,
The streaming hair, the tie behind,
The coat tails worn in front.

I marked the absent-minded scream,   13
The little nervous trick
Of rolling in the grate, with eyes
By friendship's light made quick.

But youth's black storms are gone and past,   17
Bare is each aged brow;
And, since with age we're growing bald,
Let us be babies now.

Learning we knew; but still to-day,   21
With spelling-book devotion,
Words of one syllable we seek
In moments of emotion.

Riches we knew; and well dressed dolls—   25
Dolls living—who expressed
No filial thoughts, however much
You thumped them in the chest.

Old happiness is grey as we,
    And we may still outstrip her;
If we be slippered pantaloons,
    Oh let us hunt the slipper!

                                                               29

The old world glows with colours clear;
    And if, as saith the saint,
The world is but a painted show,
    Oh let us lick the paint!

     33

Far, far behind are morbid hours,
    And lonely hearts that bleed.
Far, far behind us are the days,
    When we were old indeed.

     37

Leave we the child: he is immersed
    With scientists and mystics:
With deep prophetic voice he cries
    Canadian food statistics.

     41

But now I know how few and small,
    The things we crave need be—
Toys and the universe and you—
    A little friend to tea.

     45

Behold the simple sum of things,
    Where, in one splendour spun,
The stars go round the Mulberry Bush,
    The Burning Bush, the Sun.

     49

Now we are old and wise and grey,
    And shaky at the knees;
Now is the true time to delight
    In picture books like these.

     53

Hoary and bent I dance one hour:
    What though I die at morn?
There is a shout among the stars,
    "To-night a child is born."

     57

The Oneness of the Philosopher with Nature

I love to see the little stars
  All dancing to one tune;
I think quite highly of the Sun,
  And kindly of the Moon.

The million forests of the Earth
   Come trooping in to tea.
The great Niagara waterfall
   Is never shy with me.

I am the tiger's confidant,
  And never mention names:
The lion drops the formal "Sir,"
  And lets me call him James.

Into my ear the blushing Whale
  Stammers his love. I know
Why the Rhinoceros is sad,
  —Ah, child! 'twas long ago.

I am akin to all the Earth
    By many a tribal sign:
The aged Pig will often wear
    That sad, sweet smile of mine.

My niece, the Barnacle, has got
  My piercing eyes of black;
The Elephant has got my nose,
  I do not want it back.

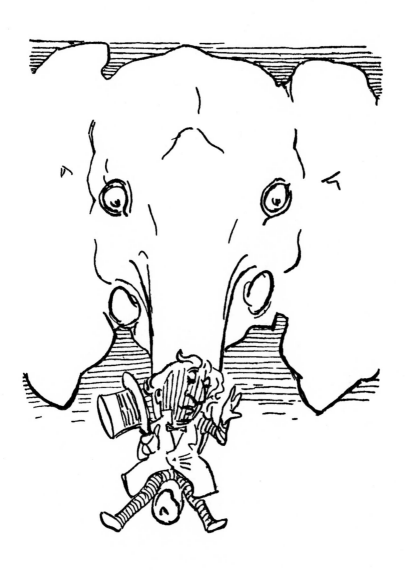

I know the strange tale of the Slug;
  The Early Sin—the Fall—
The Sleep—the Vision—and the Vow—
  The Quest—the Crown—the Call.

G. K. Chesterton's Early Poetry

And I have loved the Octopus,
   Since we were boys together.
I love the Vulture and the Shark:
   I even love the weather.

I love to bask in sunny fields,
   And when that hope is vain,
I go and bask in Baker Street,
   All in the pouring rain.

Come snow! where fly, by some strange law, 37
   Hard snowballs—without noise—
Through streets untenanted, except
   By good unconscious boys.

Come fog! exultant mystery—
  Where in strange darkness rolled,
The end of my own nose becomes
  A lovely legend old.

Come snow, and hail, and thunderbolts,
  Sleet, fire, and general fuss;
Come to my arms, come all at once—
  Oh photograph me thus!

G. K. Chesterton's Early Poetry

On the Problems Attending Altruism on the High Seas

Observe these Pirates bold and gay,
  That sail a gory sea:
Notice their bright expression:—
  The handsome one is me.

We plundered ships and harbours,   5
  We spoiled the Spanish main;
But Nemesis watched over us,
  For it began to rain.

Oh all well-meaning folk take heed!   9
  Our Captain's fate was sore;
A more well-meaning Pirate,
  Had never dripped with gore.

The rain was pouring long and loud,
    The sea was drear and dim;
A little fish was floating there:
    Our Captain pitied him.

"How sad," he said, and dropped a tear
    Splash on the cabin roof,
"That we are dry, while he is there
    Without a waterproof.

"We'll get him up on board at once;
    For Science teaches me,
He will be wet if he remains
    Much longer in the sea."

They fished him out; the First Mate wept,
    And came with rugs and ale:
The Boatswain brough him one golosh,
    And fixed it on his tail.

But yet he never loved the ship; 29
   Against the mast he'd lean;
If spoken to, he coughed and smiled,
   And blushed a pallid green.

Though plied with hardbake, beef and beer, 33
   He showed no wish to sup:
The neatest riddles they could ask,
   He always gave them up.

They seized him and court-martialled him, 37
  In some excess of spleen,
For lack of social sympathy,
  (Victoria xii. 18).

They gathered every evidence 41
  That might remove a doubt:
They wrote a postcard in his name,
  And partly scratched it out.

Till, when his guilt was clear as day, 45
  With all formality
They doomed the traitor to be drowned,
  And threw him in the sea.

The flashing sunset, as he sank,
Made every scale a gem;
And, turning with a graceful bow,
He kissed his fin to them.

G. K. Chesterton's Early Poetry

Moral

I am, I think I have remarked,   *53*
   Terrifically old,
(The second Ice-age was a farce,
   The first was rather cold.)

A friend of mine, a trilobite   *57*
   Had gathered in his youth,
When trilobites *were* trilobites,
   This all-important truth.

We aged ones play solemn parts—   *61*
   Sire—guardian—uncle—king.
Affection is the salt of life,
   Kindness a noble thing.

The old alone may comprehend   *65*
   A sense in my decree;
But—if you find a fish on land,
   Oh throw it into the sea.

On the Disastrous Spread of Æstheticism in All Classes

*I*mpetuously I sprang from bed,
Long before lunch was up,
That I might drain the dizzy dew
From day's first golden cup.

In swift devouring ecstacy   5
   Each toil in turn was done;
I had done lying on the lawn
   Three minutes after one.

For me, as Mr. Wordsworth says,   9
   The duties shine like stars;
I formed my uncle's character;
   Decreasing his cigars.

But could my kind engross me? No!   13
   Stern Art—what sons escape her?
Soon I was drawing Gladstone's nose
   On scraps of blotting paper.

Then on—to play one-fingered tunes 17
   Upon my aunt's piano.
In short, I have a headlong soul,
   I much resemble Hanno.

(Forgive the entrance of the not 21
   Too cogent Carthaginian.
It may have been to make a rhyme;
   I lean to that opinion).

G. K. Chesterton's Early Poetry

Then my great work of book research 25
   Till dusk I took in hand—
The forming of a final, sound
   Opinion on *The Strand*.

But when I quenched the midnight oil, 29
   And closed *The Referee*,
Whose thirty volumes folio
   I take to bed with me,

I had a rather funny dream, 33
   Intense, that is, and mystic;
I dreamed that, with one leap and yell,
   The world became artistic.

The Shopman, when their souls were still, 37
Declined to open shops—

And Cooks recorded frames of mind
  In sad and subtle chops.

The stars were weary of routine: 41
  The trees in the plantation
Were growing every fruit at once,
  In search of a sensation.

The moon went for a moonlight stroll,   45
  And tried to be a bard,
And gazed enraptured at itself:
  I left it trying hard.

The sea had nothing but a mood
   Of 'vague ironic gloom,'
With which t'explain its presence in
   My upstairs drawing-room.

The sun had read a little book 53
    That struck him with a notion:
He drowned himself and all his fires
    Deep in the hissing ocean.

Then all was dark, lawless, and lost: 57
    I heard great devilish wings:
I knew that Art had won, and snapt
    The Covenant of Things.

I cried aloud, and I awoke,   *61*
  New labours in my head.
I set my teeth, and manfully
  Began to lie in bed.

Toiling, rejoicing, sorrowing,   *65*
  So I my life conduct.
Each morning see some task begun,
  Each evening see it chucked.

But still, in sudden moods of dusk,   *69*
  I hear those great weird wings,
Feel vaguely thankful to the vast
  Stupidity of things.

Envoy

Clear was the night: the moon was young:
　　The larkspurs in the plots
Mingled their orange with the gold
　　Of the forget-me-nots.

The poppies seemed a silver mist:　　　　　5
　　So darkly fell the gloom.
You scarce had guessed yon crimson streaks
　　Were buttercups in bloom.

But one thing moved: a little child　　　　9
　　Crashed through the flower and fern:
And all my soul rose up to greet
　　The sage of whom I learn.

I looked into his awful eyes:　　　　　　13
　　I waited his decree:
I made ingenious attempts
　　To sit upon his knee.

The babe upraised his wondering eyes,　　17
　　And timidly he said,
"A trend towards experiment
　　In modern minds is bred.

"I feel the will to roam, to learn　　　21
　　By test, by experience, *nous*,
That fire is hot and oceans deep,
　　And wolves carnivorous.

"My brain demands complexity."   25
    The lisping cherub cried.
I looked at him, and only said,
    "Go on. The world is wide."

A tear rolled down his pinafore,   29
    "Yet from my life must pass
The simple love of sun and moon,
    The old games in the grass;

"Now that my back is to my home   33
    Could these again be found?"
I looked on him, and only said,
    "Go on. The world is round."

THE WILD KNIGHT
AND OTHER POEMS

by

G. K. CHESTERTON

Another tattered rhymster in the ring,
  With but the old plea to the sneering schools,
That on him too, some secret night in spring
  Came the old frenzy of a hundred fools

To make some thing: the old want dark and deep,   5
  The thirst of men, the hunger of the stars,
Since first it tinged even the Eternal's sleep,
  With monstrous dreams of trees and towns and
    wars.

When all He made for the first time He saw,   9
  Scattering stars as misers shake their pelf.
Then in the last strange wrath broke His own law,
  And made a graven image of Himself.

By the Babe Unborn

If trees were tall and grasses short,
  As in some crazy tale,
If here and there a sea were blue
  Beyond the breaking pale,

If a fixed fire hung in the air
  To warm me one day through,
If deep green hair grew on great hills,
  I know what I should do.

In dark I lie: dreaming that there
  Are great eyes cold or kind,
And twisted streets and silent doors,
  And living men behind.

Let storm-clouds come: better an hour,
  And leave to weep and fight,
Than all the ages I have ruled
  The empires of the night.

I think that if they gave me leave
  Within that world to stand,
I would be good through all the day
  I spent in fairyland.

They should not hear a word from me
  Of selfishness or scorn,
If only I could find the door,
  If only I were born.

The World's Lover

My eyes are full of lonely mirth:
  Reeling with want and worn with scars,
For pride of every stone on earth,
  I shake my spear at all the stars.

A live bat beats my crest above,   5
  Lean foxes nose where I have trod,
And on my naked face the love
  Which is the loneliness of God.

Outlawed: since that great day gone by—   9
  When before prince and pope and queen
I stood and spoke a blasphemy—
  'Behold the summer leaves are green.'

They cursed me: what was that to me   13
  Who in that summer darkness furled,
With but an owl and snail to see,
  Had blessed and conquered all the world?

They bound me to the scourging-stake,   17
  They laid their whips of thorn on me;
I wept to see the green rods break,
  Though blood be beautiful to see.

Beneath the gallows' foot abhorred   21
  The crowds cry 'Crucify!' and 'Kill!'
Higher the priests sing, 'Praise the Lord,
  The warlock dies'; and higher still

Shall heaven and earth hear one cry sent 25
 Even from the hideous gibbet height,
'Praise to the Lord Omnipotent,
 The vultures have a feast to-night.'

THE SKELETON

Chattering finch and water-fly
 Are not merrier than I;
Here among the flowers I lie
Laughing everlastingly.
No: I may not tell the best;
Surely, friends, I might have guessed
Death was but the good King's jest,
 It was hid so carefully.

A CHORD OF COLOUR

My Lady clad herself in grey,
 That caught and clung about her throat;
Then all the long grey winter day
 On me a living splendour smote;
And why grey palmers holy are,
 And why grey minsters great in story,
And grey skies ring the morning star,
 And grey hairs are a crown of glory.

My Lady clad herself in green, 9
 Like meadows where the wind-waves pass;
Then round my spirit spread, I ween,
 A splendour of forgotten grass.

Then all that dropped of stem or sod,
 Hoarded as emeralds might be,
I bowed to every bush, and trod
 Amid the live grass fearfully.

My Lady clad herself in blue,   17
 Then on me, like the seer long gone,
The likeness of a sapphire grew,
 The throne of him that sat thereon.
Then knew I why the Fashioner
 Splashed reckless blue on sky and sea;
And ere 'twas good enough for her,
 He tried it on Eternity.

Beneath the gnarled old Knowledge-tree   25
 Sat, like an owl, the evil sage:
'The World's a bubble,' solemnly
 He read, and turned a second page.
'A bubble, then, old crow,' I cried,
 'God keep you in your weary wit!
'A bubble—have you ever spied
 'The colours I have seen on it?'

THE HAPPY MAN

To teach the grey earth like a child,
 To bid the heavens repent,
I only ask from Fate the gift
 Of one man well content.

Him will I find: though when in vain 5
  I search the feast and mart,
The fading flowers of liberty,
  The painted masks of art.

I only find him at the last, 9
  On one old hill where nod
Golgotha's ghastly trinity—
  Three persons and one god.

THE UNPARDONABLE SIN

I do not cry, beloved, neither curse.
  Silence and strength, these two at least are good.
He gave me sun and stars and ought He could,
  But not a woman's love; for that is hers.

He sealed her heart from sage and questioner— 5
  Yea, with seven seals, as he has sealed the grave.
And if she give it to a drunken slave,
  The Day of Judgment shall not challenge her.

Only this much: if one, deserving well, 9
  Touching your thin young hands and making suit,
Feel not himself a crawling thing, a brute,
  Buried and bricked in a forgotten hell;

Prophet and poet be he over sod, 13
  Prince among angels in the highest place,
God help me, I will smite him on the face,
  Before the glory of the face of God.

A Novelty

Why should I care for the Ages
    Because they are old and grey?
To me, like sudden laughter,
    The stars are fresh and gay;
The world is a daring fancy,
    And finished yesterday.

Why should I bow to the Ages
    Because they were drear and dry?
Slow trees and ripening meadows
    For me go roaring by,
A living charge, a struggle
    To escalade the sky.

The eternal suns and systems,
    Solid and silent all,
To me are stars of an instant,
    Only the fires that fall
From God's good rocket, rising
    On this night of carnival.

Ultimate

The vision of a haloed host
    That weep around an empty throne;
And, aureoles dark and angels dead,
    Man with his own life stands alone.

'I am,' he says his bankrupt creed;
    'I am,' and is again a clod:

The sparrow starts, the grasses stir,
  For he has said the name of God.

THE DONKEY

When fishes flew and forests walked
    And figs grew upon thorn,
Some moment when the moon was blood
  Then surely I was born;

With monstrous head and sickening cry   5
  And ears like errant wings,
The devil's walking parody
  On all four-footed things.

The tattered outlaw of the earth,   9
  Of ancient crooked will;
Starve, scourge, deride me: I am dumb,
  I keep my secret still.

Fools! For I also had my hour;   13
  One far fierce hour and sweet:
There was a shout about my ears,
  And palms before my feet.

THE BEATIFIC VISION

Through what fierce incarnations, furled
    In fire and darkness, did I go,
Ere I was worthy in the world
  To see a dandelion grow?

Well, if in any woes or wars   5
   I bought my naked right to be,
Grew worthy of the grass, nor gave
   The wren, my brother, shame for me.

But what shall God not ask of him   9
   In the last time when all is told,
Who saw her stand beside the hearth,
   The firelight garbing her in gold?

The Hope of the Streets

The still sweet meadows shimmered: and I stood
   And cursed them, bloom of hedge and bird of
     tree,
And bright and high beyond the hunch-backed wood
   The thunder and the splendour of the sea.

Give back the Babylon where I was born,   5
   The lips that gape give back, the hands that grope,
And noise and blood and suffocating scorn
   An eddy of fierce faces—and a hope

That 'mid those myriad heads one head find place,   9
   With brown hair curled like breakers of the sea,
And two eyes set so strangely in the face
   That all things else are nothing suddenly.

Ecclesiastes

There is one sin: to call a green leaf grey,
   Whereat the sun in heaven shuddereth.

There is one blasphemy: for death to pray,
    For God alone knoweth the praise of death.

There is one creed: 'neath no world-terror's wing   5
    Apples forget to grow on apple-trees.
There is one thing is needful—everything—
    The rest is vanity of vanities.

The Song of the Children

The World is ours till sunset,
    Holly and fire and snow;
And the name of our dead brother
    Who loved us long ago.

The grown folk mighty and cunning,   5
    They write his name in gold;
But we can tell a little
    Of the million tales he told.

He taught them laws and watchwords,   9
    To preach and struggle and pray;
But he taught us deep in the hayfield
    The games that the angels play.

Had he stayed here for ever,   13
    Their world would be wise as ours—
And the king be cutting capers,
    And the priest be picking flowers.

But the dark day came: they gathered: 17
    On their faces we could see

They had taken and slain our brother,
    And hanged him on a tree.

THE FISH

Dark the sea was: but I saw him,
    One great head with goggle eyes,
Like a diabolic cherub
    Flying in those fallen skies.

I have heard the hoarse deniers,   5
    I have known the wordy wars;
I have seen a man, by shouting,
    Seek to orphan all the stars.

I have seen a fool half-fashioned   9
    Borrow from the heavens a tongue,
So to curse them more at leisure—
    —And I trod him not as dung.

For I saw that finny goblin   13
    Hidden in the abyss untrod;
And I knew there can be laughter
    On the secret face of God.

Blow the trumpets, crown the sages,   17
    Bring the age by reason fed!
('He that sitteth in the heavens,
    'He shall laugh'—the prophet said.)

Gold Leaves

*L*o! I am come to autumn,
  When all the leaves are gold;
Grey hairs and golden leaves cry out
  The year and I are old.

In youth I sought the prince of men,   5
  Captain in cosmic wars,
Our Titan, even the weeds would show
  Defiant, to the stars.

But now a great thing in the street   9
  Seems any human nod,
Where shift in strange democracy
  The million masks of God.

In youth I sought the golden flower   13
  Hidden in wood or wold,
But I am come to autumn,
  When all the leaves are gold.

Thou Shalt Not Kill

I had grown weary of him; of his breath
  And hands and features I was sick to death.
Each day I heard the same dull voice and tread;
I did not hate him: but I wished him dead.
And he must with his blank face fill my life—
Then my brain blackened, and I snatched a knife.

But ere I struck, my soul's grey deserts through   7
A voice cried, 'Know at least what thing you do.'
This is a common man: knowest thou, O soul,
'What this thing is? somewhere where seasons roll
'There is some living thing for whom this man
'Is as seven heavens girt into a span,
'For some one soul you take the world away—
'Now know you well your deed and purpose. Slay!'

Then I cast down the knife upon the ground   15
And saw that mean man for one moment crowned.
I turned and laughed: for there was no one by—
The man that I had sought to slay was I.

A Certain Evening

That night the whole world mingled,
   The souls were babes at play,
And angel danced with devil,
   And God cried, 'Holiday!'

The sea had climbed the mountain peaks,   5
   And shouted to the stars
To come to play: and down they came
   Splashing in happy wars.

The pine grew apples for a whim,   9
   The cart-horse built a nest;
The oxen flew, the flowers sang,
   The sun rose in the west.

And 'neath the load of many worlds,   13
   The lowest life God made
Lifted his huge and heavy limbs
   And into heaven strayed.

To where the highest life God made   17
   Before His presence stands;
But God himself cried, 'Holiday!'
   And she gave me both her hands.

A MAN AND HIS IMAGE

All day the nations climb and crawl and pray
   In one long pilgrimage to one white shrine,
Where sleeps a saint whose pardon, like his peace,
   Is wide as death, as common, as divine.

His statue in an aureole fills the shrine,   5
   The reckless nightingale, the roaming fawn,
Share the broad blessing of his lifted hands,
   Under the canopy, above the lawn.

But one strange night, a night of gale and flood,   9
   A sound came louder than the wild wind's tone;
The grave-gates shook and opened: and one stood
   Blue in the moonlight, rotten to the bone.

Then on the statue, graven with holy smiles,   13
   There came another smile—tremendous—one
Of an Egyptian god. 'Why should you rise?
   'Do I not guard your secret from the sun?

'The nations come; they kneel among the flowers   17
    Sprung from your blood, blossoms of May and June,
Which do not poison them—is it not strange?
    Speak!' And the dead man shuddered in the moon.

'Shall I not cry the truth?'—the dead man cowered—
    'Is it not sad, with life so tame and cold,
That earth should fade into the sun's white fires
    With the best jest in all its tales untold?

'If I should cry that in this shrine lie hid   25
    Stories that Satan from his mouth would spew;
Wild tales that men in hell tell hoarsely—speak!
    Saint and Deliverer! Should I slander you?'

Slowly the cowering corse reared up its head,   29
    'Nay, I am vile . . . but when for all to see,
You stand there, pure and painless—death of life!
    Let the stars fall—I say you slander me!

'You make me perfect, public, colourless;   33
    You make my virtues sit at ease—you lie!
For mine were never easy—lost or saved,
    I had a soul—I was. And where am I?

'Where is my good? the little real hoard,   37
    The secret tears, the sudden chivalries;
The tragic love, the futile triumph—where?
    Thief, dog, and son of devils—where are these?

'I will lift up my head: in leprous loves   41
    Lost, and the soul's dishonourable scars—

The Wild Knight and Other Poems   55

By God I was a better man than This
   That stands and slanders me to all the stars.

'Come down!' And with an awful cry, the corse   45
   Sprang on the sacred tomb of many tales,
And stone and bone, locked in a loathsome strife,
   Swayed to the singing of the nightingales.

Then one was thrown: and where the statue stood   49
   Under the canopy, above the lawn,
The corse stood; grey and lean, with lifted hands
   Raised in tremendous welcome to the dawn.

'Now let all nations climb and crawl and pray;   53
   Though I be basest of my old red clan,
They shall not scale, with cries or sacrifice,
   The stature of the spirit of a man.'

THE MARINER

The violet scent is sacred
   Like dreams of angels bright;
The hawthorn smells of passion
   Told in a moonless night.

But the smell is in my nostrils,   5
   Through blossoms red or gold,
Of my own green flower unfading,
   A bitter smell and bold.

The lily smells of pardon,   9
   The rose of mirth; but mine

Smells shrewd of death and honour,
    And the doom of Adam's line.

The heavy scent of wine-shops   13
    Floats as I pass them by,
But never a cup I quaff from,
    And never a house have I.

Till dropped down forty fathoms,   17
    I lie eternally;
And drink from God's own goblet
    The green wine of the sea.

The Triumph of Man

*I*plod and peer amid mean sounds and shapes,
  I hunt for dusty gain and dreary praise,
    And slowly pass the dismal grinning days,
Monkeying each other like a line of apes.

What care? There was one hour amid all these   5
    When I had stripped off like a tawdry glove
    My starriest hopes and wants, for very love
Of time and desolate eternities.

Yea, for one great hour's triumph, not in me   9
    Nor any hope of mine did I rejoice,
    But in a meadow game of girls and boys
Some sunset in the centuries to be.

CYCLOPEAN

A mountainous and mystic brute
No rein can curb, no arrow shoot,
Upon whose domed deformèd back
I sweep the planets' scorching track.

Old is the elf, and wise, men say,   5
His hair grows green as ours grows grey;
He mocks the stars with myriad hands,
High as that swinging forest stands.

But though in pigmy wanderings dull   9
I scour the deserts of his skull,
I never find the face, eyes, teeth,
Lowering or laughing underneath.

I met my foe in an empty dell,   13
His face in the sun was naked hell.
I thought, 'One silent, bloody blow,
No priest would curse, no crowd would know.'

Then cowered: a daisy, half concealed,   17
Watched for the fame of that poor field;
And in that flower and suddenly
Earth opened its one eye on me.

JOSEPH

If the stars fell; night's nameless dreams
Of bliss and blasphemy came true,
If skies were green and snow were gold,

And you loved me as I love you;

O long light hands and curled brown hair,   5
   And eyes where sits a naked soul;
Dare I even then draw near and burn
   My fingers in the aureole?

Yes, in the one wise foolish hour   9
   God gives this strange strength to a man.
He can demand, though not deserve,
   Where ask he cannot, seize he can.

But once the blood's wild wedding o'er,   13
   Were not dread his, half dark desire,
To see the Christ-child in the cot,
   The Virgin Mary by the fire?

MODERN ELFLAND

I cut a staff in a churchyard copse,
   I clad myself in ragged things,
I set a feather in my cap
   That fell out of an angel's wings.

I filled my wallet with white stones,   5
   I took three foxgloves in my hand,
I slung my shoes across my back,
   And so I went to fairyland.

But lo, within that ancient place   9
   Science had reared her iron crown,
And the great cloud of steam went up

That telleth where she takes a town.

But cowled with smoke and starred with lamps 13
   That strange land's light was still its own;
The word that witched the woods and hills
   Spoke in the iron and the stone.

Not Nature's hand had ever curved 17
   That mute unearthly porter's spine.
Like sleeping dragon's sudden eyes
   The signals leered along the line.

The chimneys thronging crooked or straight 21
   Were fingers signalling the sky;
The dog that strayed across the street
   Seemed four-legged by monstrosity.

'In vain,' I cried, 'though you too touch 25
   The new time's desecrating hand,
Through all the noises of a town
   I hear the heart of fairyland.'

I read the name above a door, 29
   Then through my spirit pealed and passed
'This is the town of thine own home,
   And thou hast looked on it at last.'

ETERNITIES

I cannot count the pebbles in the brook.
   Well hath He spoken: 'Swear not by thy head,
   Thou knowest not the hairs,' though He, we read,

Writes that wild number in his own strange book.

I cannot count the sands or search the seas,   5
    Death cometh, and I leave so much untrod.
    Grant my immortal aureole, O my God,
And I will name the leaves upon the trees.

In heaven I shall stand on gold and glass,   9
    Still brooding earth's arithmetic to spell;
    Or see the fading of the fires of hell
Ere I have thanked my God for all the grass.

A Christmas Carol

The Christ-child lay on Mary's lap,
    His hair was like a light.
(O weary, weary were the world,
    But here is all aright.)

The Christ-child lay on Mary's breast,   5
    His hair was like a star.
(O stern and cunning are the kings,
    But here the true hearts are.)

The Christ-child lay on Mary's heart,   9
    His hair was like a fire.
(O weary, weary is the world,
    But here the world's desire.)

The Christ-child stood at Mary's knee,   13
    His hair was like a crown,
And all the flowers looked up at him.

And all the stars looked down.

ALONE

Blessings there are of cradle and of clan,
 Blessings that fall of priests' and princes' hands;
 But never blessing full of lives and lands,
Broad as the blessing of a lonely man.

Though that old king fell from his primal throne,   5
 And ate among the cattle, yet this pride
 Had found him in the deepest grass, and cried
An 'Ecce Homo' with the trumpets blown.

And no mad tyrant, with almighty ban,   9
 Who in strong madness dreams himself divine,
 But hears through fumes of flattery and of wine
The thunder of this blessing name him man.

Let all earth rot past saints' and seraphs' plea,   13
 Yet shall a Voice cry through its last lost war,
 'This is the world, this red wreck of a star,
That a man blessed beneath an alder-tree.'

KING'S CROSS STATION

This circled cosmos whereof man is god
 Has suns and stars of green and gold and red,
And cloudlands of great smoke, that range o'er range
 Far floating, hide its iron heavens o'erhead.

God! shall we ever honour what we are,   5
 And see one moment ere the age expire,

The vision of man shouting and erect,
   Whirled by the shrieking steeds of flood and fire?

Or must Fate act the same grey farce again,   9
   And wait, till one, amid Time's wrecks and scars,
Speaks to a ruin here, 'What poet-race
   Shot such cyclopean arches at the stars?'

THE HUMAN TREE

Many have Earth's lovers been,
   Tried in seas and wars, I ween;
Yet the mightiest have I seen:
   Yea, the best saw I.
One that in a field alone
Stood up stiller than a stone
Lest a moth should fly.

Birds had nested in his hair,   8
On his shoon were mosses rare,
Insect empires flourished there,
   Worms in ancient wars;
But his eyes burn like a glass,
Hearing a great sea of grass
   Roar towards the stars.

From them to the human tree   15
Rose a cry continually,
'Thou art still, our Father, we
   Fain would have thee nod.
Make the skies as blood below thee,

Though thou slay us, we shall know thee.
    Answer us, O God!

'Show thine ancient flame and thunder,   22
Split the stillness once asunder,
Lest we whisper, lest we wonder
    Art thou there at all?'
But I saw him there alone,
Standing stiller than a stone
    Lest a moth should fall.

To Them that Mourn

(W.E.G., May 1898)

*L*ift up your heads: in life, in death,
    God knoweth his head was high.
Quit we the coward's broken breath
    Who watched a strong man die.

If we must say, 'No more his peer   5
    Cometh; the flag is furled.'
Stand not too near him, lest he hear
    That slander on the world.

The good green earth he loved and trod   9
    Is still, with many a scar,
Writ in the chronicles of God,
    A giant-bearing star.

He fell: but Britain's banner swings   13
    Above his sunken crown.

Black death shall have his toll of kings
  Before that cross goes down.

Once more shall move with mighty things   17
  His house of ancient tale,
Where kings whose hands were kissed of kings
  Went in: and came out pale.

O young ones of a darker day,   21
  In art's wan colours clad,
Whose very love and hate are grey—
  Whose very sin is sad.

Pass on: one agony long-drawn   25
  Was merrier than your mirth,
When hand-in-hand came death and dawn,
  And spring was on the earth.

THE OUTLAW

Priest, is any song-bird stricken?
  Is one leaf less on the tree?
Is this wine less red and royal
  That the hangman waits for me?

He upon your cross that hangeth,   5
  It is writ of priestly pen,
On the night they built his gibbet,
  Drank red wine among his men.

Quaff, like a brave man, as he did,   9
  Wine and death as heaven pours—

This is my fate: O ye rulers,
   O ye pontiffs, what is yours?

To wait trembling, lest yon loathly
   Gallows-shape whereon I die,
In strange temples yet unbuilded,
   Blaze upon an altar high.

BEHIND

I saw an old man like a child,
  His blue eyes bright, his white hair wild,
Who turned for ever, and might not stop,
Round and round like an urchin's top.

'Fool,' I cried, 'while you spin round,
'Others grow wise, are praised, are crowned.'
Ever the same round road he trod,
'This is better: I seek for God.'

'We see the whole world, left and right,
'Yet at the blind back hides from sight
'The unseen Master that drives us forth
'To East and West, to South and North.

'Over my shoulder for eighty years
I have looked for the gleam of the sphere of spheres.'
'In all your turning, what have you found?'
'At least, I know why the world goes round.'

The End of Fear

Through the whole heaven be one-eyed with the
    moon,
  Though the dead landscape seem a thing possessed,
  Yet I go singing through that land oppressed
As one that singeth through the flowers of June.

No more, with forest-fingers crawling free
  O'er dark flint wall that seems a wall of eyes,
  Shall evil break my soul with mysteries
Of some world-poison maddening bush and tree.

No more shall leering ghosts of pimp and king
  With bloody secrets veiled before me stand.
  Last night I held all evil in my hand
Closed and behold it was a little thing.

I broke the infernal gates and looked on him
  Who fronts the strong creation with a curse;
  Even the god of a lost universe,
Smiling above his hideous cherubim.

And pierced far down in his soul's crypt unriven
  The last black crooked sympathy and shame,
  And hailed him with that ringing rainbow name
Erased upon the oldest book in heaven.

Like emptied idiot masks, sin's loves and wars
  Stare at me now: for in the night I broke
  The bubble of a great world's jest, and woke
Laughing with laughter such as shakes the stars.

The Holy of Holies

'Elder father, though thine eyes
Shine with hoary mysteries,
Canst thou tell what in the heart
Of a cowslip blossom lies?

'Smaller than all lives that be,   5
Secret as the deepest sea,
Stands a little house of seeds,
Like an elfin's granary.

'Speller of the stones and weeds,   9
Skilled in Natures craft's and creeds,
Tell me what is in the heart
Of the smallest of the seeds.'

'God Almighty, and with Him   13
Cherubim and Seraphim,
Filling all eternity—
Adonai Elohim.'

The Mirror of Madmen

I dreamed a dream of heaven, white as frost,
The splendid stillness of a living host;
Vast choirs of upturned faces, line o'er line.
Then my blood froze; for every face was mine.

Spirits with sunset plumage throng and pass,   5
Glassed darkly in the sea of gold and glass.
But still on every side, in every spot,

I saw a million selves, who saw me not.

I fled to quiet wastes, where on a stone,   9
Perchance, I found a saint, who sat alone;
I came behind: he turned with slow, sweet grace,
And faced me with my happy, hateful face.

I cowered like one that in a tower doth bide,   13
Shut in by mirrors upon every side;
Then I saw, islanded in skies alone
And silent, one that sat upon a throne.

His robe was bordered with rich rose and gold,   17
Green, purple, silver out of sunsets old;
But o'er his face a great cloud edged with fire,
Because it covereth the world's desire.

But as I gazed, a silent worshipper,   21
Methought the cloud began to faintly stir;
Then I fell flat, and screamed with grovelling head,
'If thou hast any lightning, strike me dead!

'But spare a brow where the clean sunlight fell,   25
The crown of a new sin that sickens hell.
Let me not look aloft and see mine own
Feature and form upon the Judgment-throne.'

Then my dream snapped: and with a heart that leapt 29
I saw across the tavern where I slept,
The sight of all my life most full of grace,
A gin-damned drunkard's wan half-witted face.

E. C. B.

*B*efore the grass grew over me,
  I knew one good man through and through,
And knew a soul and body joined
  Are stronger than the heavens are blue.

A wisdom worthy of thy joy,   5
  O great heart, read I as I ran;
Now, though men smite me on the face,
  I cannot curse the face of man.

I loved the man I saw yestreen   9
  Hanged with his babe's blood on his palms.
I loved the man I saw to-day
  Who knocked not when he came with alms.

Hush!—for thy sake I even faced   13
  The knowledge that is worse than hell;
And loved the man I saw but now
  Hanging head downwards in the well.

THE DESECRATERS

*W*itness all: that unrepenting,
  Feathers flying, music high,
I go down to death unshaken
  By your mean philosophy.

For your wages, take my body,   5
  That at least to you I leave;
Set the sulky plumes upon it,

Bid the grinning mummers grieve.

Stand in silence: steep your raiment 9
  In the night that hath no star;
Don the mortal dress of devils,
  Blacker than their spirits are.

Since ye may not, of your mercy, 13
  Ere I lie on such a hearse,
Hurl me to the living jackals
  God hath built for sepulchres.

AN ALLIANCE

This is the weird of a world-old folk,
  That not till the last link breaks,
Not till the night is blackest,
  The blood of Hengist wakes.
When the sun is black in heaven,
  The moon as blood above,
And the earth is full of hatred,
  This people tells its love.

In change, eclipse, and peril, 9
  Under the whole world's scorn,
By blood and death and darkness
  The Saxon peace is sworn;
That all our fruit be gathered,
  And all our race take hands,
And the sea be a Saxon river
  That runs through Saxon lands.

Lo! not in vain we bore him 17
   Behold it! not in vain,
Four centuries' dooms of torture
   Choked in the throat of Spain,
Ere priest or tyrant triumph—
   We know how well—we know—
Bone of that bone can whiten,
   Blood of that blood can flow.

Deep grows the hate of kindred, 25
   Its roots take hold on hell;
No peace or praise can heal it,
   But a stranger heals it well.
Seas shall be red as sunsets,
   And kings' bones float as foam,
And heaven be dark with vultures,
   The night our son comes home.

THE ANCIENT OF DAYS

A child sits in a sunny place,
   Too happy for a smile,
And plays through one long holiday
   With balls to roll and pile;
A painted wind-mill by his side
   Runs like a merry tune,
But the sails are the four great winds of heaven,
   And the balls are the sun and moon.

A staring doll's-house shows to him   9
    Green floors and starry rafter,
And many-coloured graven dolls
    Live for his lonely laughter.
The dolls have crowns and aureoles,
    Helmets and horns and wings,
For they are the saints and seraphim,
    The prophets and the kings.

THE LAST MASQUERADE

A wan new garment of young green
    Touched, as you turned your soft brown hair
    And in me surged the strangest prayer
Ever in lover's heart hath been.

That I who saw your youth's bright page,   5
    A rainbow change from robe to robe,
    Might see you on this earthly globe,
Crowned with the silver crown of age.

Your dear hair powdered in strange guise,   9
    Your dear face touched with colours pale;
    And gazing through the mask and veil
The mirth of your immortal eyes.

THE EARTH'S SHAME

Name not his deed: in shuddering and in haste
    We dragged him darkly o'er the windy fell:
That night there was a gibbet in the waste,

And a new sin in hell.

Be his deed hid from commonwealths and kings,   5
   By all men born be one true tale forgot;
But three things, braver than all earthly things,
      Faced him and feared him not.

Above his head and sunken secret face   9
   Nested the sparrow's young and dropped not dead.
From the red blood and slime of that lost place
      Grew daisies white, not red.

And from high heaven looking upon him,   13
   Slowly upon the face of God did come
A smile the cherubim and seraphim
      Hid all their faces from.

VANITY

A wan sky greener than the lawn,
   A wan lawn paler than the sky.
She gave a flower into my hand,
   And all the hours of eve went by.

Who knows what round the corner waits   5
   To smite? If shipwreck, snare, or slur
Shall leave me with a head to lift,
   Worthy of him that spoke with her.

A wan sky greener than the lawn,   9
   A wan lawn paler than the sky.
She gave a flower into my hand,

And all the days of life went by.

Live ill or well, this thing is mine, 13
  From all I guard it, ill or well.
One tawdry, tattered, faded flower
  To show the jealous kings in hell.

The Lamp Post

Laugh your best, O blazoned forests,
  Me ye shall not shift or shame
With your beauty: here among you
  Man hath set his spear of flame.

Lamp to lamp we send the signal, 5
  For our lord goes forth to war;
Since a voice, ere stars were builded,
  Bade him colonise a star.

Laugh ye, cruel as the morning, 9
  Deck your heads with fruit and flower,
Though our souls be sick with pity,
  Yet our hands are hard with power.

We have read your evil stories, 13
  We have heard the tiny yell
Through the voiceless conflagration
  Of your green and shining hell.

And when men, with fires and shouting, 17
  Break your old tyrannic pales;
And where ruled a single spider

Laugh and weep a million tales.

This shall be your best of boasting: 21
  That some poet, poor of spine,
Full and sated with our wisdom,
  Full and fiery with our wine,

Shall steal out and make a treaty   25
  With the grasses and the showers,
Rail against the grey town-mother,
  Fawn upon the scornful flowers;

Rest his head among the roses,   29
  Where a quiet song-bird sounds,
And no sword made sharp for traitors,
  Hack him into meat for hounds.

The Pessimist

You that have snarled through the ages, take your
    answer and go—
I know your hoary question, the riddle that all men
    know.
You have weighed the stars in a balance, and grasped
    the skies in a span
Take, if you must have answer, the word of a common
    man.

Deep in my life lies buried one love unhealed,
    unshriven,   5
One hunger still shall haunt me—yea, in the streets of
    heaven;

This is the burden, babbler, this is the curse shall cling,
This is the thing I bring you; this is the pleasant thing.

'Gainst you and all your sages, no joy of mine shall
    strive,   9
This one dead self shall shatter the men you call alive.
My grief I send to smite you, no pleasure, no belief,
Lord of the battered grievance, what do you know of
    grief?

I only know the praises to heaven that one man gave, 13
That he came on earth for an instant, to stand beside a
    grave,
The peace of a field of battle, where flowers are born of
    blood.
I only know one evil that makes the whole world good.

Beneath this single sorrow the globe of moon and
    sphere   17
Turns to a single jewel, so bright and brittle and dear
  That I dread lest God should drop it, to be dashed
    into stars below.

    .   .   .   .

You that have snarled through the ages, take your
    answer and go.

A Fairy Tale

All things grew upwards, foul and fair:
    The great trees fought and beat the air
With monstrous wings that would have flown;

But the old earth clung to her own,
Holding them back from heavenly wars,
Though every flower sprang at the stars.

But he broke free: while all things ceased, 7
Some hour increasing, he increased.
The town beneath him seemed a map,
Above the church he cocked his cap,
Above the cross his feather flew
Above the birds: and still he grew.

The trees turned grass; the clouds were riven; 13
His feet were mountains lost in heaven;
Through strange new skies he rose alone,
The earth fell from him like a stone,
And his own limbs beneath him far
Seemed tapering down to touch a star.

He reared his head, shaggy and grim, 19
Staring among the cherubim;
The seven celestial floors he rent,
One crystal dome still o'er him bent:
Above his head, more clear than hope,
All heaven was a microscope.

A Portrait

Fair faces crowd on Christmas night
   Like seven suns a-row,
But all beyond is the wolfish wind
   And the crafty feet of the snow.

But through the rout one figure goes   5
  With quick and quiet tread;
Her robe is plain, her form is frail—
  Wait if she turn her head.

I say no word of line or hue,   9
  But if that face you see,
Your soul shall know the smile of faith's
  Awful frivolity.

Know that in this grotesque old masque   13
  Too loud we cannot sing,
Or dance too wild, or speak too wide
  To praise a hidden thing.

That though the jest be old as night,   17
  Still shaketh sun and sphere
An everlasting laughter
  Too loud for us to hear.

FEMINA CONTRA MUNDUM

The sun was black with judgment, and the moon
      Blood: but between
I saw a man stand, saying, 'To me at least
      The grass is green.

'There was no star that I forgot to fear   5
      With love and wonder.
The birds have loved me'; but no answer came—
      Only the thunder.

. . . .

Once more the man stood, saying, 'A cottage door,   *9*
      Wherethrough I gazed
That instant as I turned—yea, I am vile;
      Yet my eyes blazed.

'For I had weighed the mountains in a balance,   *13*
      And the skies in a scale,
I come to sell the stars—old lamps for new—
      Old stars for sale.'

Then a calm voice fell all the thunder through,   *17*
      A tone less rough:
'Thou hast begun to love one of my works
      Almost enough.'

To a Certain Nation

We will not let thee be, for thou art ours.
  We thank thee still, though thou forget these
    things,
For that hour's sake when thou didst wake all powers
  With a great cry that God was sick of kings.

Leave thee there grovelling at their rusted greaves,   *5*
  These hulking cowards on a painted stage,
Who, with imperial pomp and laurel leaves,
  Show their Marengo—one man in a cage.

These, for whom stands no type or title given   *9*
  In all the squalid tales of gore and pelf;

      G. K. Chesterton's Early Poetry

Though cowed by crashing thunders from all heaven,
   Cain never said, 'My brother slew himself.'

Tear you the truth out of your drivelling spy,   13
   The maniac whom you set to swing death's scythe.
Nay; torture not the torturer—let him lie:
   What need of racks to teach a worm to writhe?

Bear with us, O our sister, not in pride,   17
   Nor any scorn we see thee spoiled of knaves,
But only shame to hear, where Danton died,
   Thy foul dead kings all laughing in their graves.

Thou hast a right to rule thyself; to be   21
   The thing thou wilt; to grin, to fawn, to creep
To crown these clumsy liars; ay, and we
   Who knew thee once, we have a right to weep.

The Praise of Dust

'What of vile dust?' the preacher said.
   Methought the whole world woke,
The dead stone lived beneath my foot,
   And my whole body spoke.

'You, that play tyrant to the dust,   5
   And stamp its wrinkled face,
This patient star that flings you not
   Far into homeless space.

'Come down out of your dusty shrine   9
   The living dust to see,

The flowers that at your sermon's end
　Stand blazing silently.

'Rich white and blood-red blossom; stones,　　　13
　Lichens like fire encrust;
A gleam of blue, a glare of gold,
　The vision of the dust.

'Pass them all by: till, as you come　　　17
　Where, at a city's edge,
Under a tree—I know it well—
　Under a lattice ledge,

'The sunshine falls on one brown head.　　　21
　You, too, O cold of clay,
Eater of stones, may haply hear
　The trumpets of that day

'When God to all his paladins　　　25
　By his own splendour swore
To make a fairer face than heaven.
　Of dust and nothing more.'

THE BALLAD OF
THE BATTLE OF GIBEON

Five kings rule o'er the Amorite,
　　Mighty as fear and old as night;
Swathed with unguent and gold and jewel,
Waxed they merry and fat and cruel.
Zedek of Salem, a terror and glory,
Whose face was hid while his robes were gory;
And Hoham of Hebron, whose loathly face is
Heavy and dark o'er the ruin of races;
And Piram of Jarmuth, drunk with strange wine,
Who dreamed he had fashioned all stars that shine;
And Debir of Eglon wild, without pity,
Who raged like a plague in the midst of his city;
And Japhia of Lachish, a fire that flameth,
Who did in the daylight what no man nameth.

These five kings said one to another,　　　　　15
'King unto king o'er the world is brother,
Seeing that now, for a sign and a wonder,
A red eclipse and a tongue of thunder,
A shape and a finger of desolation,
Is come against us a kingless nation.
Gibeon hath failed us: it were not good
That a man remember where Gibeon stood.'
Then Gibeon sent to our captain, crying,
'Son of Nun, let a shaft be flying,
For unclean birds are gathering greedily;

Slack not thy hand, but come thou speedily.
Yea, we are lost save thou maintain'st us,
For the kings of the mountains are gathered against
    us.'

Then to our people spake the Deliverer,   29
'Gibeon is high, yet a host may shiver her;
Gibeon hath sent to me crying for pity,
For the lords of the cities encompass the city
With chariot and banner and bowman and lancer,
And I swear by the living God I will answer.
Gird you, O Israel, quiver and javelin,
Shield and sword for the road we travel in,
Verily, as I have promised, pay I
Life unto Gibeon, death unto Ai.'

Sudden and still as a bolt shot right   39
Up on the city we went by night.
Never a bird of the air could say,
'This was the children of Israel's way.'
Only the hosts sprang up from sleeping,
Saw from the heights a dark stream sweeping;
Sprang up straight as a great shout stung them,
And heard the Deliverer's war-cry among them,
Heard under cupola, turret, and steeple
The awful cry of the kingless people.

Started the weak of them, shouted the strong of them,
Crashed we a thunderbolt into the throng of them,   50
Blindly with heads bent, and shields forced before us,

We heard the dense roar of the strife closing o'er us.
And drunk with the crash of the song that it sung
    them,
We drove the great spear-blade in God's name among
    them.

Redder and redder the sword-flash fell,   55
Our eyes and our nostrils were hotter than hell;
Till full all the crest of the spear-surge shocking us,
Hoham of Hebron cried out mocking us,
'Nay, what need of the war-sword's plying,
Out of the desert the dust comes flying.
A little red dust, if the wind be blowing—
Who shall reek of its coming or going?'
Back the Deliverer spake as a clarion,
'Mock at thy slaves, thou eater of carrion!
Laughest thou at us, in thy kingly clowning,
We, that laughed upon Ramases frowning,
We that stood up proud, unpardoned,
When his face was dark and his heart was hardened?
Pharaoh we knew and his steeds, not faster
Than the word of the Lord in thine ear, O master.
Sheer through the turban his wantons wove him,
Clean to the skull the Deliverer clove him;
And the two hosts reeled at the sign appalling,
As the great king fell like a great house falling.

Loudly we shouted, and living and dying, 75
Bore them all backward with strength and strong
      crying;
And Caleb struck Zedek hard at the throat,
And Japhia of Lachish Zebulon smote.
The war-swords and axes were clashing and groaning,
The fallen were fighting and foaming and moaning,
The war-spears were breaking, the war-horns were
      braying,
Ere the hands of the slayers were sated with slaying.
And deep in the grasses grown gory and sodden,
The treaders of all men were trampled and trodden;
And over them, routed and reeled like cattle,
High over the turn of the tide of the battle,
High over noises that deafen and cover us,
Rang the Deliverer's voice out over us.

'Stand thou still, thou sun upon Gibeon, 89
Stand thou, moon, in the valley of Ajalon!
Shout thou, people, a cry like thunder,
For the kings of the earth are broken asunder.
Now we have said as the thunder says it,
Something is stronger than strength and slays it.
Now we have written for all time later,
Five kings are great, yet a law is greater.
Stare, O sun! in thine own great glory,
This is the turn of the whole world's story.
Stand thou still, thou sun upon Gibeon,
Stand thou, moon, in the valley of Ajalon!

G. K. Chesterton's Early Poetry

'Smite! amid spear-blades blazing and breaking,   101
More than we know of is rising and making.
Stab with the javelin, crash with the car!
Cry! for we know not the thing that we are.
Stand, O sun! that in horrible patience
Smiled on the smoke and the slaughter of nations.
Thou shalt grow sad for a little crying,
Thou shalt be darkened for one man's dying—
Stand thou still, thou sun upon Gibeon,
Stand thou, moon, in the valley of Ajalon!'

After the battle was broken and spent   111
Up to the hill the Deliverer went,
Flung up his arms to the storm-clouds flying,
And cried unto Israel, mightily crying,
'Come up, O warriors! come up, O brothers!
Tribesmen and herdsmen, maidens and mothers;
The bondman's son and the bondman's daughter,
The hewer of wood and the drawer of water,
He that carries and he that brings,
And set your foot on the neck of kings.'

This is the story of Gibeon fight—   121
Where we smote the lords of the Amorite;
Where the banners of princes with slaughter were
        sodden,
And the beards of seers in the rank grass trodden;
Where the trees were wrecked by the wreck of cars,
And the reek of the red field blotted the stars;

Where the dead heads dropped from the swords that
    sever,
Because His mercy endureth for ever.

'VULGARIZED'

All round they murmur, 'O profane,
    Keep thy heart's secret hid as gold';
But I, by God, would sooner be
    Some knight in shattering wars of old,

In brown outlandish arms to ride,   5
    And shout my love to every star
With lungs to make a poor maid's name
    Deafen the iron ears of war.

Here, where these subtle cowards crowd,   9
    To stand and so to speak of love,
That the four corners of the world
    Should hear it and take heed thereof.

That to this shrine obscure there be   13
    One witness before all men given,
As naked as the hanging Christ,
    As shameless as the sun in heaven.

These whimperers—have they spared to us   17
    One dripping woe, one reeking sin?
These thieves that shatter their own graves
    To prove the soul is dead within.

They talk; by God, is it not time 21
   Some of Love's chosen broke the girth,
And told the good all men have known
   Since the first morning of the earth?

THE BALLAD OF
THE GOD-MAKERS

A bird flew out at the break of day
   From the nest where it had curled
And ere the eve the bird had set
   Fear on the kings of the world.

The first tree it lit upon   5
   Was green with leaves unshed;
The second tree it lit upon
   Was red with apples red;

The third tree it lit upon   9
   Was barren and was brown,
Save for a dead man nailed thereon
   On a hill above a town.

That night the kings of the earth were gay   13
   And filled the cup and can;
Last night the kings of the earth were chill
   For dread of a naked man.

'If he speak two more words,' they said,   17
   'The slave is more than the free;
'If he speak three more words,' they said,

'The stars are under the sea.'

Said the King of the East to the King of the West,   21
   I wot his frown was set,
'Lo, let us slay him and make him as dung,
   It is well that the world forget.'

Said the King of the West to the King of the East,   25
   I wot his smile was dread,
'Nay, let us slay him and make him a god,
   It is well that our god be dead.'

They set the young man on a hill,   29
   They nailed him to a rod;
And there in darkness and in blood
   They made themselves a god.

And the mightiest word was left unsaid,   33
   And the world had never a mark,
And the strongest man of the sons of men
   Went dumb into the dark.

Then hymns and harps of praise they brought,   37
   Incense and gold and myrrh,
And they thronged above the seraphim,
   The poor dead carpenter.

'Thou art the prince of all,' they sang,   41
   'Ocean and earth and air.'
Then the bird flew on to the cruel cross,
   And hid in the dead man's hair.

'Thou art the sun of the world,' they cried,   45
  'Speak if our prayers be heard.'
And the brown bird stirred in the dead man's hair,
  And it seemed that the dead man stirred.

Then a shriek went up like the world's last cry   49
  From all nations under heaven,
And a master fell before a slave
  And begged to be forgiven.

They cowered, for dread in his wakened eyes   53
  The ancient wrath to see;
And the bird flew out of the dead Christ's hair,
  And lit on a lemon-tree.

AT NIGHT

How many million stars there be,
  That only God hath numbered;
But this one only chosen for me
In time before her face was fled.
Shall not one mortal man alive
        Hold up his head?

THE WOOD CUTTER

We came behind him by the wall,
  My brethren drew their brands,
And they had strength to strike him down—
  And I to bind his hands.

Only once, to a lantern gleam,
    He turned his face from the wall,
And it was as the accusing angel's face
    On the day when the stars shall fall.

I grasped the axe with shaking hands,
    I stared at the grass I trod;
For I feared to see the whole bare heavens
    Filled with the face of God.

I struck: the serpentine slow blood
    In four arms soaked the moss—
Before me, by the living Christ,
    The blood ran in a cross.

Therefore I toil in forests here
    And pile the wood in stacks,
And take no fee from the shivering folk
    Till I have cleansed the axe.

But for a curse God cleared my sight,
    And where each tree doth grow
I see a life with awful eyes,
    And I must lay it low.

ART COLOURS

On must we go: we search dead leaves,
    We chase the sunset's saddest flames,
The nameless hues that o'er and o'er
    In lawless wedding lost their names.

God of the daybreak! Better be   5
  Black savages; and grin to gird
Our limbs in gaudy rags of red,
  The laughing-stock of brute and bird;

And feel again the fierce old feast,   9
  Blue for seven heavens that had sufficed,
A gold like shining hoards, a red
  Like roses from the blood of Christ.

The Two Women

*L*o! very fair is she who knows the ways
  Of joy: in pleasure's mocking wisdom old,
The eyes that might be cold to flattery, kind;
  The hair that might be grey with knowledge, gold.

But thou art more than these things, O my queen,   5
  For thou art clad in ancient wars and tears.
And looking forth, framed in the crown of thorns,
  I saw the youngest face in all the spheres.

Good News

*B*etween a meadow and a cloud that sped
  In rain and twilight, in desire and fear,
  I heard a secret—hearken in your ear,
'Behold the daisy has a ring of red.'

That hour, with half of blessing, half of ban,   5
  A great voice went through heaven and earth and
    hell,

Crying, 'We are tricked, my great ones, is it well?
Now is the secret stolen by a man.'

Then waxed I like the wind because of this,   9
  And ran, like gospel and apocalypse,
  From door to door, with new anarchic lips,
Crying the very blasphemy of bliss.

In the last wreck of Nature, dark and dread,   13
  Shall in eclipse's hideous hieroglyph,
  One wild form reel on the last rocking cliff,
And shout, 'The daisy has a ring of red.'

THE WILD KNIGHT

The wasting thistle whitens on my crest,
  The barren grasses blow upon my spear,
A green, pale pennon: blazon of wild faith
And love of fruitless things: yea, of my love,
Among the golden loves of all the knights,   5
Alone: most hopeless, sweet, and blasphemous,
The love of God:

               I hear the crumbling creeds

Like cliffs washed down by water, change, and pass;
I hear a noise of words, age after age,   10
A new cold wind that blows across the plains,
And all the shrines stand empty; and to me
All these are nothing: priests and schools may doubt
Who never have believed; but I have loved.
Ah friends, I know it passing well, the love   15
Wherewith I love; it shall not bring to me
Return or hire or any pleasant thing—
Ay, I have tried it: Ay, I know its roots.
Earthquake and plague have burst on it in vain
And rolled back shattered—   20

               Babbling neophytes!

Blind, startled fools—think you I know it not?
Think you to teach me? Know I not His ways?
Strange-visaged blunders, mystic cruelties.
All! all! I know Him, for I love Him. Go!   25

So, with the wan waste grasses on my spear,
I ride for ever, seeking after God.
My hair grows whiter than my thistle plume,
And all my limbs are loose; but in my eyes
The star of an unconquerable praise: 30
For in my soul one hope for ever sings,
That at the next white corner of a road
My eyes may look on Him. . . .

Hush—I shall know

The place when it is found: a twisted path 35
Under a twisted pear-tree—this I saw
In the first dream I had ere I was born,
Wherein He spoke. . . .

But the grey clouds come down

In hail upon the icy plains: I ride, 40
Burning for ever in consuming fire.

*A dark manor-house shuttered and unlighted,
outlined against a pale sunset: in front a large, but
neglected, garden. To the right, in the foreground,
the porch of a chapel, with coloured windows
lighted. Hymns within.*

*Above the porch a grotesque carved bracket,
supporting a lantern. Astride of it sits Captain
Redfeather, a flagon in his hand.*

REDFEATHER.

I have drunk to all I know of,

To every leaf on the tree,
To the highest bird of the heavens,
To the lowest fish of the sea.
What toast, what toast remaineth,
Drunk down in the same good wine,
By the tippler's cup in the tavern,
And the priest's cup at the shrine?

    *A Priest comes out, stick in hand, and looks right
    and left.]*

VOICES WITHIN.

The brawler . . .

PRIEST

    He has vanished

REDFEATHER.

To the stars.

[The Priest looks up.]

PRIEST [*Angrily*].

What would you there, sir?

REDFEATHER.

Give you all a toast.

[Lifts his flagon. More priests come out.]

I see my life behind me: bad enough—
Drink, duels, madness, beggary, and pride,
The life of the unfit: yet ere I drop

On Nature's rubbish heap, I weigh it all,
And give you all a toast—

[Reels to his feet and stands.]

The health of God!

[They all recoil from him.]

Let's give the Devil of the Heavens His due!
He that made grass so green, and wine so red,
Is not so black as you have painted him.

[Drinks.]

PRIEST.

Blaspheming profligate!

REDFEATHER [hurls the flagon among them.]
Howl! ye dumb dogs,
I named your King—let me have one great shout,
Flutter the seraphim like startled birds;
Make God recall the good days of His youth
Ere saints had saddened Him: when He came back
Conqueror of Chaos in a six days' war,
With all the sons of God shouting for joy . . .

PRIEST.

And you—what is your right, and who are you,
To praise God?

REDFEATHER.

A lost soul. In earth or heaven

What has a better right?

PRIEST.

Go, pagan, go!
Drink, dice, and dance: take no more thought than
    blind
Beasts of the field. . . .

REDFEATHER.

Or . . . lilies of the field,
To quote a pagan sage. I go my way.

PRIEST [*solemnly*].
And when Death comes . . .

REDFEATHER.

He shall not find me dead.

[*Puts on his plumed hat. The priests go out.*]

REDFEATHER.
These frozen fools . . .

[*The Lady Olive comes out of the chapel. He sees
her.*]

Oh, they were right enough,
Where shall I hide my carrion from the sun?

[*Buries his face. His hat drops to the ground.*]

OLIVE [*looking up*].
Captain, are you from church? I saw you not.

Redfeather.

No, I am here.

[Lays his hand on a gargoyle.]

I, too, am a grotesque,
And dance with all the devils on the roof.

Olive *[with a strange smile]*.

For Satan, also, I have often prayed.

Redfeather *[roughly]*.

Satan may worry women if he will,
For he was but an angel ere he fell,
But I—before I fell—I was a man.

Olive.

He too, my Master, was a man: too strong
To fear a strong man's sins: 'tis written He
Descended into hell.

Redfeather.

Write, then, that I

[Leaps to the ground before her.]

Descended into heaven . . .

You are ill?

Olive.

No, well . . .

Redfeather.

You speak the truth—you are the Truth—

Lady, say once again then, 'I am *well.*'

OLIVE.

I—ah! God give me grace—I am nigh dead.

REDFEATHER [*quietly*].

Lord Orm?

OLIVE.

Yes—yes.

REDFEATHER.

Is in your father's house—
Having the title-deeds—would drive you forth,
Homeless, and with your father sick to death,
Into this winter, save on a condition
Named . . .

OLIVE.

And unnameable. Even so; Lord Orm—
Ah! do you know him?

REDFEATHER.

Ay, I saw him once.
The sun shone on his face, that smiled and smiled,
A sight not wholesome to the eyes of man.

OLIVE.

Captain, I tell you God once fell asleep,
And in that hour the world went as it would;
Dogs brought forth cats, and poison grew in grapes,
And Orm was born . . .

REDFEATHER.

Why, curse him! can he not
Be kicked or paid?

OLIVE [*feverishly*].

Hush! He is just behind
There in the house—see how the great house glares,
Glares like an ogre's mask—the whole dead house
Possessed with bestial meaning. . . .

[*Screams.*]

Ah! the face!
The whole great grinning house—his face! his face!
His face!

REDFEATHER [*in a voice of thunder, pointing away from
the house*].

Look there—look there!

OLIVE.

What is it? What?

REDFEATHER.

I think it was a bird.

OLIVE.

What thought you, truly?

REDFEATHER.

I think a mighty thought is drawing near.

[Enter The Wild Knight.]

THE WILD KNIGHT.

That house . . .

[Points.]

OLIVE.

Ah Christ! *[Shudders.]* I had forgotten it.

THE WILD KNIGHT *[still pointing]*.

That house! the house at last, the house of God,
Wherein God makes an evening feast for me.
The house at last: I know the twisted path
Under the twisted pear-tree: this I saw
In the first dream I had ere I was born.
It is the house of God. He welcomes me.

[Strides forward.]

REDFEATHER.

That house. God's blood!

OLIVE *[hysterically]*.

Is not this hell's own wit?

THE WILD KNIGHT.

God grows impatient, and His wine is poured,
His bread is broken.

[Rushes forward.]

REDFEATHER [*leaps between*].

Stand away, great fool,

There is a devil there!

THE WILD KNIGHT [*draws his sword, and waves it as he rushes*].

God's house!—God's house!

REDFEATHER [*plucks out his own sword*].

Better my hand than his.

[*The blades clash.*]

God alone knows

What That within might do to you, poor fool,
I can but kill you.

[*They fight. Olive tries to part them.*]

REDFEATHER.

Olive, stand away!

OLIVE.

I will not stand away!

[*Steps between the swords.*]

Stranger, a word,

Yes—you are right—God is within that house.

REDFEATHER.

Olive!

OLIVE.

But He is all too beautiful
For us who only know of stars and flowers.
The thing within is all too pure and fair,

[Shudders.]

Too awful in its ancient innocence,
For men to look upon it and not die;
Ourselves would fade into those still white fires
Of peace and mercy.

[Struggles with her voice.]

There . . . enough . . . the law—
No flesh shall look upon the Lord and live.

REDFEATHER [sticking his sword in the ground].
You are the bravest lady in the world.

THE WILD KNIGHT [dazed].
May I not go within?

REDFEATHER.

Keep you the law—
No flesh shall look upon the Lord and live.

THE WILD KNIGHT [sadly].
Then I will go and lay me in the flowers,
For He may haply, as in ancient time,
Walk in the garden in the cool of day.

[He goes out.]

[Olive reels. Redfeather catches her.]

REDFEATHER.

You are the strongest woman upon earth.
The weakest woman than the strongest man
Is stronger in her hour: this is the law.
When the hour passes—then may we be strong.

OLIVE [*wildly*].

The House . . . the Face.

REDFEATHER [*fiercely*].

I love you. Look at me!

OLIVE [*turns her face to him*].

I hear six birds sing in that little tree,
Say, is the old earth laughing at my fears?
I think I love you also . . .

REDFEATHER.

What I am

You know. But I will never curse a man,
Even in a mirror.

OLIVE [*smiling at him*].

And the Devil's dance?

REDFEATHER.

The Devil plotted since the world was young
With alchemies of fire and witches' oils
And magic. But he never made a man.

OLIVE.

No, not a man.

REDFEATHER.

Not even my Lord Orm.

Look at the house now—

[She starts and looks.]

Honest brick and tiles.

OLIVE.

You have a strange strength in this hour.

REDFEATHER.

This hour

I see with mortal eye as in one flash
The whole divine democracy of things,
And dare the stars to scorn a scavenge-heap.
Olive, I tell you every soul is great.
Weave we green crowns—how noble and how high;
Fling we white flowers—how radiant and how pure.
Is he, whoe'er lie be, who next shall cross
This scrap of grass . . .

[Enter Lord Orm.]

OLIVE [screams].

Ah!

REDFEATHER [pointing to the chapel].

Olive, go and pray

For a man soon to die. Good-day, my Lord.

    [She goes in.]

LORD ORM.

Good-day.

REDFEATHER.

I am a friend to Lady Olive.

LORD ORM.

Sir, you are fortunate.

REDFEATHER.

Most fortunate

In finding, sword on thigh and ready, one
Who is a villain and a gentleman.

LORD ORM [*picks up the flagon*].

Empty, I see.

REDFEATHER.

Oh sir, you never drink.

You dread to lose yourself before the stars—
Do you not dread to sleep?

LORD ORM [*violently*].

What would you here?

REDFEATHER.

Receive from you the title-deeds you hold.

LORD ORM.

You entertain me.

REDFEATHER.

With a bout at foils?

LORD ORM.

I will not fight.

REDFEATHER.

I know you better, then.
I have seen men grow mangier than the beasts,
Eat bread with blood upon their fingers, grin
While women burned: but one last law they served.
When I say 'Coward,' is the law awake?

LORD ORM.

Hear me, then, too: I have seen robbers rule,
And thieves go clad in gold—age after age—
Because, though sordid, ragged, rude, and mean,
They saw, like gods, no law above their heads.
But when they fell—then for this cause they fell,
This last mean cobweb of the fairy tales
Of good and ill: that they must stand and fight
When a man bade, though they had chose to stand
And fight not. I am stronger than the world.

  [Folds his arms.]

REDFEATHER [lifts his hand].
If in your body be the blood of man,

  [Strikes him.]

Now let it rush to the face—

                              God! Have you sunk
Lower than anger?

                    LORD ORM.

                              How I triumph now.

          REDFEATHER [*stamps wildly*].
Damned, whimpering dog! vile, snivelling, sick
     poltroon!
Are you alive?

                    LORD ORM.

                         Evil, be thou my good;
Let the sun blacken and the moon be blood:
I have said the words.

               REDFEATHER [*studying him*].

                         And if I struck you dead,
You would turn to daisies!

                    LORD ORM.

                         And you do not strike.

          REDFEATHER [*dreamily*].
Indeed, poor soul, such magic would be kind
And full of pity as a fairy-tale:
One touch of this bright wand [*Lifts his sword*] and
     down would drop
The dark abortive blunder that is you,
And you would change, forgiven, into flowers.

Lord Orm.

And yet—and yet you do not strike me dead.
I do not draw: the sword is in your hand—
Drive the blade through me where I stand.

Redfeather.

Lord Orm.

You asked the Lady Olive (I can speak
As to a toad to you, my lord)—you asked
Olive to be your paramour: and she—

Lord Orm.

Refused.

Redfeather.

And yet her father was at stake,
And she is soft and kind. Now look at me,
Ragged and ruined, soaked in bestial sins:
My lord, I too have my virginity—
Turn the thing round, my lord, and topside down.
You cannot spell it. Be the fact enough,
I use no sword upon a swordless man.

Lord Orm.

For her?

Redfeather.

I too have my virginity.

Lord Orm.

Now look on me: I am the lord of earth,
For I have broken the last bond of man.

The Wild Knight and Other Poems 111

I stand erect, crowned with the stars—and why?
Because I stand a coward—because you
Have mercy—on a coward. Do I win?

> REDFEATHER.

Though there you stand with moving mouth and eyes,
I think, my lord, you are not possible—
God keep you from my dreams.

　[*Goes out.*]

> LORD ORM.

　　　　　　　　　　　Alone and free.

Since first in flowery meads a child I ran,
My one long thirst—to be alone and free.
Free of all laws, creeds, codes, and common tests,
Shameless, anarchic, infinite.

　　　　　　　　　　　　　Why, then,

I might have done in that dark liberty—
If I should say 'a good deed,' men would laugh,
But here are none to laugh.

　　　　　　　　　　　　The godless world

Be thanked there is no God to spy on me,
Catch me and crown me with a vulgar crown
For what I do: if I should once believe
The horror of that ancient Eavesdropper
Behind the starry arras of the skies,
I should—well, well, enough of menaces—

I should not do the thing I come to do.
What do I come to do? Let me but try
To spell it to my soul.

Suppose a man

Perfectly free and utterly alone,
Free of all love of law, equally free
Of all the love of mutiny it breeds,
Free of the love of heaven, and also free
Of all the love of hell it drives us to;
Not merely void of rules, unconscious of them;
So strong that naught alive could do him hurt,
So wise that he knew all things, and so great
That none knew what he was or what he did—
A lawless giant.

[A pause: then in a low voice.]

Would he not be good?
Hate is the weakness of a thwarted thing,
Pride is the weakness of a thing unpraised.
But he, this man . . .

He would be like a child
Girt with the tomes of some vast library,
Who reads romance after romance, and smiles
When every tale ends well: impersonal
As God he grows—melted in suns and stars;
So would this boundless man, whom none could spy,
Taunt him with virtue, censure him with vice,

Rejoice in all men's joys; with golden pen
Write all the live romances of the earth
To a triumphant close . . .

Alone and free—

In this grey, cool, clean garden, washed with winds,
What do I come to do among the grass,
The daisies, and the dews? An awful thing,
To prove I am that man.

That while these saints

Taunt me with trembling, dare me to revenge,
I breathe an upper air of ancient good
And strong eternal laughter; send my sun
And rain upon the evil and the just,
Turn my left cheek unto the smiter. He
That told me, sword in hand, that I had fallen
Lower than anger, knew not I had risen
Higher than pride . . .

Enough, the deeds are mine.

[Takes out the title-deeds.]

I come to write the end of a romance.
A good romance: the characters—Lord Orm,
Type of the starvéd heart and storéd brain,
Who strives to hate and cannot; fronting him—
Redfeather rake in process of reform,
At root a poet: I have hopes of him:

He can love virtue, for he still loves vice.
He is not all burnt out. He beats me there
(How I beat him in owning it!); in love
He is still young, and has the joy of shame.
And for the Lady Olive—who shall speak?
A man may weigh the courage of a man,
But if there be a bottomless abyss
It is a woman's valour: such as I
Can only bow the knee and hide the face
(Thank God there is no God to spy on me
And bring his curséd crowns).

                                    No, there is none:
The old incurable hunger of the world
Surges in wolfish wars, age after age.
There was no God before me: none sees where,
Between the brute-womb and the deaf, dead grave,
Unhoping, unrecorded, unrepaid,
I make with smoke, fire, and burnt-offering
This sacrifice to Chaos. [*Lights the papers.*] None
    behold
Me write in fire the end of the romance.
Burn! I am God, and crown myself with stars
Upon creation day: before was night
And chaos of a blind and cruel world.
I am the first God; I will trample hell,
Fight, conquer, make the story of the stars,
Like this poor story, end like a romance:

[*The paper burns.*]

Before was brainless night: but I am God
In this black world I rend. Let there be light!

[*The paper blazes up, illuminating the garden.*]

I, God . . .

THE WILD KNIGHT [*rushes forward*].

God's Light! God's Voice; yes, it is He
Walking in Eden in the cool of the day!

LORD ORM [*screams*].

Tricked! Caught!
Damned screeching rat in a hole!

[*Stabs him again and again with his sword;
stamps on his face.*]

The Wild Knight [*faintly*].

Earth grows too beautiful around me: shapes
And colours fearfully wax fair and clear,
For I have heard, as thro' a door ajar,
Scraps of the huge soliloquy of God
That moveth as a mask the lips of man.
If man be very silent: they were right,
No flesh shall look upon the Lord and live.

[*Dies*]

LORD ORM [*staggers back laughing*].

Saved, saved, my secret.

REDFEATHER [*rushing in, sword in hand*].

                    The drawn sword at last!
Guard, son of hell!

  [*They fight. Orm falls. Olive comes in.*]

                    He too can die. Keep back!
Olive, keep back from him! I did not fear
Him living, and he fell before my sword;
But dead I fear him. All is ended now;
A man's whole life tied in a bundle there,
And no good deed. I fear him. Come away.

THE BALLAD OF THE
WHITE HORSE

by

G. K. CHESTERTON

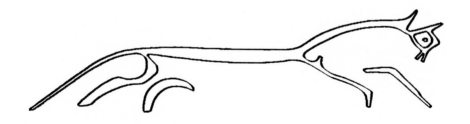

"I say, as do all Christian men, that it is a
divine purpose that rules and not fate."

King Alfred's addition to Boethius

INTRODUCTION:
THE BALLAD OF THE WHITE HORSE

It was one of the darkest moments in World War II. On June 1, 1941 the island of Crete fell to a German airborne invasion, and no less than 17,000 British troops became prisoners of war. To express the feelings of the nation, on its front page *The Times* of London ran these words from Chesterton's *The Ballad of the White Horse:*

"I tell you naught for your comfort,
    Yea, naught for your desire,
Save that the sky grows darker yet
    And the sea rises higher."

The quote was apt, for Chesterton's great epic describes King Alfred's struggle to defend a Christian England against an invasion by pagan Danes. And, although rooted in history, as Chesterton noted in the first sentence of his "Prefactory Note," his tale was not intended as a mere recital of events. Instead, he wove into one grand epic the local legends that had grown up around King Alfred, a genuine historical figure, and his desperate 878 A.D battle with the Danes. Even the source of Alfred's vision expresses the grimness of the times. Unlike many Catholic stories, when Mary says the words above, she is not offering assurance. She is playing the traditional role of woman urging a man she loves to fight, perhaps to the death, for what they both hold dear.

Chesterton was doing with English history what J. R. R. Tolkien would later do with his invented history of Middle-earth. They created a tradition (Chesterton) or a mythology (Tolkien) that saw history not as mere events but as a story of cosmic significance. That's the reason for the quote on the title page: "I say, as do all Christian men, that it is a divine purpose that rules, and not fate." The author was the King Alfred of this tale, in an addition he made to his Old English translation of Boethius' *The Consolation of Philosophy*.

Chesterton described the contrary (and wrong) point of view in the fifth chapter of his *Eugenics and Other Evils*:

> The mark of the atheistic [literary] style is that it instinctively chooses the word which suggests that things are dead things: that things have no souls. Thus they will not speak of waging war, which means willing it; they speak of the 'outbreak of war,' as if all the guns blew up without the men touching them.

In this tale, responding to a divine vision, King Alfred most emphatically wills war and does so with no assurance of victory. In her contribution to *Celebrating Middle-earth*, Janet Blumberg notes a similar theme in Tolkien:

> When you think of the legacy of what Tolkien absorbed from Anglo-Saxon literature, then think of a dark and fatalistic worldview that does not fear darkness or run away from the battle. Even in defeat, what matters is *mod*—the inward goodness that gleams out more strongly ("*mod* shall be the more") when we are being overwhelmed and defeated. All human beings know about "the great temporal defeat," but not all know or trust in a faithfulness that transcends death.

Tolkien believed each of us plays a role in history. In a May 1944 letter he told his son Christopher, "You are inside a very great story!" and urged him to be worthy of it. He expressed the idea more clearly in a July 1956 letter, when he wrote about a leading character in *The Lord of the Rings*:

Frodo deserved all honour because he spent every drop of his power of will and body, and that was just sufficient to bring him to the destined point, and no further.... The Other Power then took over, the Writer of the Story (by which I do not mean myself), "that ever present Person who is never absent and never named" (as one critic has said).

Chesterton knew the real Battle of Ethandune was fought near Edington, but chose for literary reasons to place it in Berkshire close to the Uffington White Horse for whom his tale was named. It is the oldest and best known of the roughly fifty white horses cut into English hills. Chesterton believed it to be very old ("Before the gods that made the gods"). Archaelogical research (*Uffington White Horse and its Landscape*) has shown he was right, with the most probable date of construction between 1200 and 800 B.C.

If not cared for, the horse would have been covered by weeds in a generation or two. So for some three thousand years, local residents have faithfully weeded and repaired it, as Chesterton knew (Bk. III, lines 32f & 362f). He even has King Alfred "bade them keep the White Horse white" (VIII, 133f) as a symbol that in this troubled world, "terror and theft " must be fought and defeated time after time (VIII, 178f). Note too the warning that in "some far century" the danger to England will come not from invading warriors, but from those who order "all things with dead words.... And Man no more a free Knight, that loves or hates his Lord."

With that I leave you to enjoy Chesterton's marvelous tale of faith and courage.

Michael W. Perry, Seattle, September 11, 2004

Prefatory Note

This ballad needs no historical notes, for the simple reason that it does not profess to be historical. All of it that is not frankly fictitious, as in any prose romance about the past, is meant to emphasize tradition rather than history. King Alfred is not a legend in the sense that King Arthur may be a legend; that is, in the sense that he may possibly be a lie. But King Alfred is a legend in this broader and more human sense, that the legends are the most important things about him.

The cult of Alfred was a popular cult, from the darkness of the ninth century to the deepening twilight of the twentieth. It is wholly as a popular legend that I deal with him here. I write as one ignorant of everything, except that I have found the legend of a King of Wessex still alive in the land. I will give three curt cases of what I mean. A tradition connects the ultimate victory of Alfred with the valley in Berkshire called the Vale of the White Horse. I have seen doubts of the tradition, which may be valid doubts. I do not know when or where the story started; it is enough that it started somewhere and ended with me; for I only seek to write upon a hearsay, as the old balladists did. For the second case, there is a popular tale that Alfred played the harp and sang in the Danish camp; I select it because it is a popular tale, at whatever time it arose. For the third case, there is a popular tale that Alfred came in contact with a woman and cakes; I select it because it is a popular tale, because it is a vulgar one. It has been disputed by grave historians, who were, I think, a little too grave to be good judges of it. The two chief charges against the story are that it was first recorded long after

Alfred's death, and that (as Mr. Oman urges) Alfred never really wandered all alone without any thanes or soldiers. Both these objections might possibly be met. It has taken us nearly as long to learn the whole truth about Byron, and perhaps longer to learn the whole truth about Pepys, than elapsed between Alfred and the first writing of such tales. And as for the other objection, do the historians really think that Alfred after Wilton, or Napoleon after Leipsic, never walked about in a wood by himself for the matter of an hour or two? Ten minutes might be made sufficient for the essence of the story. But I am not concerned to prove the truth of these popular traditions. It is enough for me to maintain two things: that they are popular traditions; and that without these popular traditions we should have bothered about Alfred about as much as we bother about Eadwig.

One other consideration needs a note. Alfred has come down to us in the best way (that is, by national legends) solely for the same reason as Arthur and Roland and the other giants of that darkness, because he fought for the Christian civilization against the heathen nihilism. But since this work was really done by generation after generation, by the Romans before they withdrew, and by the Britons while they remained, I have summarised this first crusade in a triple symbol, and given to a fictitious Roman, Celt, and Saxon, a part in the glory of Ethandune. I fancy that in fact Alfred's Wessex was of very mixed bloods; but in any case, it is the chief value of legend to mix up the centuries while preserving the sentiment; to see all ages in a sort of splendid foreshortening. That is the use of tradition: it telescopes history.

G.K.C.

DEDICATION

Of great limbs gone to chaos,
   A great face turned to night—
Why bend above a shapeless shroud
Seeking in such archaic cloud
   Sight of strong lords and light?

Where seven sunken Englands   6
   Lie buried one by one,
Why should one idle spade, I wonder,
Shake up the dust of thanes like thunder
   To smoke and choke the sun?

In cloud of clay so cast to heaven   11
   What shape shall man discern?
These lords may light the mystery
Of mastery or victory,
And these ride high in history,
   But these shall not return.

Gored on the Norman gonfalon   17
   The Golden Dragon died:
We shall not wake with ballad strings
The good time of the smaller things,
We shall not see the holy kings
   Ride down by Severn side.

Stiff, strange, and quaintly coloured   23
   As the broidery of Bayeux
The England of that dawn remains,

And this of Alfred and the Danes
Seems like the tales a whole tribe feigns
   Too English to be true.

Of a good king on an island   29
   That ruled once on a time;
And as he walked by an apple tree
There came green devils out of the sea
With sea-plants trailing heavily
   And tracks of opal slime.

Yet Alfred is no fairy tale;   35
   His days as our days ran,
He also looked forth for an hour
On peopled plains and skies that lower,
From those few windows in the tower
   That is the head of a man.

But who shall look from Alfred's hood   41
   Or breathe his breath alive?
His century like a small dark cloud
Drifts far; it is an eyeless crowd,
Where the tortured trumpets scream aloud
   And the dense arrows drive.

Lady, by one light only   47
   We look from Alfred's eyes,
We know he saw athwart the wreck
The sign that hangs about your neck,
Where One more than Melchizedek
   Is dead and never dies.

Therefore I bring these rhymes to you 53
  Who brought the cross to me,
Since on you flaming without flaw
I saw the sign that Guthrum saw
When he let break his ships of awe,
  And laid peace on the sea.

Do you remember when we went 59
  Under a dragon moon,
And 'mid volcanic tints of night
Walked where they fought the unknown fight
And saw black trees on the battle-height,
  Black thorn on Ethandune?

And I thought, "I will go with you, 65
  As man with God has gone,
And wander with a wandering star,
The wandering heart of things that are,
The fiery cross of love and war
  That like yourself, goes on."

O go you onward; where you are 71
  Shall honour and laughter be,
Past purpled forest and pearled foam,
God's winged pavilion free to roam,
Your face, that is a wandering home,
  A flying home for me.

Ride through the silent earthquake lands, 77
  Wide as a waste is wide,

Across these days like deserts, when
Pride and a little scratching pen
Have dried and split the hearts of men,
  Heart of the heroes, ride.

Up through an empty house of stars,   83
  Being what heart you are,
Up the inhuman steeps of space
As on a staircase go in grace,
Carrying the firelight on your face
  Beyond the loneliest star.

Take these; in memory of the hour   89
  We strayed a space from home
And saw the smoke-hued hamlets, quaint
With Westland king and Westland saint,
And watched the western glory faint
  Along the road to Frome.

                                        G. K. C.

Book I
The Vision of the King

Before the gods that made the gods
  Had seen their sunrise pass,
The White Horse of the White Horse Vale
  Was cut out of the grass.

Before the gods that made the gods   5
  Had drunk at dawn their fill,
The White Horse of the White Horse Vale
  Was hoary on the hill.

Age beyond age on British land,   9
  Æons on æons gone,
Was peace and war in western hills,
  And the White Horse looked on.

For the White Horse knew England   13
  When there was none to know;
He saw the first oar break or bend,
He saw heaven fall and the world end,
  O God, how long ago.

For the end of the world was long ago—   18
  And all we dwell to-day
As children of some second birth,
  Like a strange people left on earth
  After a judgment day.

For the end of the world was long ago,   23
  When the ends of the world waxed free,
When Rome was sunk in a waste of slaves,
  And the sun drowned in the sea.

When Cæsar's sun fell out of the sky   27
  And whoso hearkened right
Could only hear the plunging
  Of the nations in the night.

When the ends of the earth came marching in   31
  To torch and cresset gleam.
And the roads of the world that lead to Rome
Were filled with faces that moved like foam,
  Like faces in a dream.

And men rode out of the eastern lands,   36
  Broad river and burning plain;
Trees that are Titan flowers to see,
And tiger skies, striped horribly,
  With tints of tropic rain.

Where Ind's enamelled peaks arise   41
  Around that inmost one,
Where ancient eagles on its brink,
Vast as archangels, gather and drink
  The sacrament of the sun.

And men brake out of the northern lands,   46
  Enormous lands alone,
Where a spell is laid upon life and lust

And the rain is changed to a silver dust
  And the sea to a great green stone.

And a Shape that moveth murkily   51
  In mirrors of ice and night,
Hath blanched with fear all beasts and birds,
As death and a shock of evil words
  Blast a man's hair with white.

And the cry of the palms and the purple moons,   56
  Or the cry of the frost and foam,
Swept ever around an inmost place,
And the din of distant race on race
  Cried and replied round Rome.

And there was death on the Emperor   61
  And night upon the Pope;
And Alfred, hiding in deep grass,
  Hardened his heart with hope.

A sea-folk blinder than the sea   65
  Broke all about his land,
But Alfred up against them bare
And gripped the ground and grasped the air,
  Staggered, and strove to stand.

He bent them back with spear and spade,   70
  With desperate dyke and wall,
With foemen leaning on his shield
And roaring on him when he reeled;
  And no help came at all.

He broke them with a broken sword   75
    A little towards the sea,
And for one hour of panting peace,
Ringed with a roar that would not cease,
With golden crown and girded fleece
    Made laws under a tree.

.   .   .   .

The Northmen came about our land   81
    A Christless chivalry:
Who knew not of the arch or pen,
Great, beautiful half-witted men
    From the sunrise and the sea.

Misshapen ships stood on the deep   86
    Full of strange gold and fire,
And hairy men, as huge as sin,
With hornèd heads, came wading in
    Through the long, low sea-mire.

Our towns were shaken of tall kings   91
    With scarlet beards like blood;
The world turned empty where they trod,
They took the kindly cross of God
    And cut it up for wood.

Their souls were drifting as the sea,   96
    And all good towns and lands
They only saw with heavy eyes,
    And broke with heavy hands,

Their gods were sadder than the sea,
    Gods of a wandering will,
Who cried for blood like beasts at night,
    Sadly, from hill to hill.   *100*

They seemed as trees walking the earth,
    As witless and as tall,
Yet they took hold upon the heavens
    And no help came at all.   *104*

They bred like birds in English woods,
    They rooted like the rose,
When Alfred came to Athelney
    To hide him from their bows   *108*

There was not English armour left,
    Nor any English thing,
When Alfred came to Athelney
    To be an English king.   *112*

For earthquake swallowing earthquake
    Uprent the Wessex tree;
The whirlpool of the pagan sway
Had swirled his sires as sticks away
    When a flood smites the sea.   *116*

And the great kings of Wessex
    Wearied and sank in gore,
And even their ghosts in that great stress
Grew greyer and greyer, less and less,
With the lords that died in Lyonesse   *121*

And the king that comes no more.

And the God of the Golden Dragon 127
  Was dumb upon his throne,
And the lord of the Golden Dragon
  Ran in the woods alone.

And if ever he climbed the crest of luck 131
  And set the flag before,
Returning as a wheel returns,
Came ruin and the rain that burns,
  And all began once more.

And naught was left King Alfred 136
  But shameful tears of rage,
In the island in the river
  In the end of all his age.

In the island in the river 140
  He was broken to his knee;
And he read, writ with an iron pen,
That God had wearied of Wessex men
And given their country, field and fen,
  To the devils of the sea.

And he saw in a little picture, 146
  Tiny and far away,
His mother sitting in Egbert's hall,
And a book she showed him, very small,
Where a sapphire Mary sat in stall
  With a golden Christ at play.

It was wrought in the monk's slow manner, 152
  From silver and sanguine shell,
Where the scenes are little and terrible,
  Keyholes of heaven and hell.

In the river island of Athelney, 156
  With the river running past,
In colours of such simple creed
All things sprang at him, sun and weed,
Till the grass grew to be grass indeed
  And the tree was a tree at last.

Fearfully plain the flowers grew, 162
  Like the child's book to read,
Or like a friend's face seen in a glass;
He looked; and there Our Lady was,
She stood and stroked the tall live grass
  As a man strokes his steed.

Her face was like an open word 168
  When brave men speak and choose,
The very colours of her coat
  Were better than good news.

She spoke not, nor turned not, 172
  Nor any sign she cast,
Only she stood up straight and free,
Between the flowers in Athelney,
  And the river running past.

One dim ancestral jewel hung 177
    On his ruined armour grey,
He rent and cast it at her feet:
Where, after centuries, with slow feet,
Men came from hall and school and street
    And found it where it lay.

"Mother of God," the wanderer said, 183
    "I am but a common king,
Nor will I ask what saints may ask,
    To see a secret thing.

"The gates of heaven are fearful gates, 187
    Worse than the gates of hell;
Not I would break the splendours barred
Or seek to know the thing they guard,
    Which is too good to tell.

"But for this earth most pitiful, 192
    This little land I know,
If that which is for ever is,
Or if our hearts shall break with bliss,
    Seeing the stranger go?

"When our last bow is broken, Queen, 197
    And our last javelin cast,
Under some sad, green evening sky,
Holding a ruined cross on high,
Under warm westland grass to lie,
    Shall we come home at last?"

And a voice came human but high up, 203
   Like a cottage climbed among
The clouds; or a serf of hut and croft
That sits by his hovel fire as oft,
But hears on his old bare roof aloft
   A belfry burst in song.

"The gates of heaven are lightly locked, 209
   We do not guard our gain,
The heaviest hind may easily
Come silently and suddenly
   Upon me in a lane.

"And any little maid that walks 214
   In good thoughts apart,
May break the guard of the Three Kings
And see the dear and dreadful things
   I hid within my heart.

"The meanest man in grey fields gone 219
   Behind the set of sun,
Heareth between star and other star,
Through the door of the darkness fallen ajar,
The council, eldest of things that are,
   The talk of the Three in One.

"The gates of heaven are lightly locked, 225
   We do not guard our gold;
Men may uproot where worlds begin,
Or read the name of the nameless sin;
But if he fail or if he win

To no good man is told.

"The men of the East may spell the stars,   231
   And times and triumphs mark,
But the men signed of the cross of Christ
   Go gaily in the dark.

"The men of the East may search the scrolls   235
   For sure fates and fame,
But the men that drink the blood of God
   Go singing to their shame.

"The wise men know what wicked things   239
   Are written on the sky,
They trim sad lamps, they touch sad strings,
Hearing the heavy purple wings,
Where the forgotten seraph kings
   Still plot how God shall die.

"The wise men know all evil things   245
   Under the twisted trees,
Where the perverse in pleasure pine,
And men are weary of green wine
   And sick of crimson seas.

"But you and all the kind of Christ   250
   Are ignorant and brave,
And you have wars you hardly win
   And souls you hardly save.

"I tell you naught for your comfort,   254
   Yea, naught for your desire,

Save that the sky grows darker yet
　　And the sea rises higher.

"Night shall be thrice night over you,　　258
　　And heaven an iron cope.
Do you have joy without a cause,
　　Yea, faith without a hope?"

Even as she spoke she was not,　　262
　　Nor any word said he,
He only heard, still as he stood
Under the old night's nodding hood,
The sea-folk breaking down the wood
　　Like a high tide from sea.

He only heard the heathen men,　　268
　　Whose eyes are blue and bleak,
Singing about some cruel thing
Done by a great and smiling king
　　In daylight on a deck.

He only heard the heathen men,　　273
　　Whose eyes are blue and blind,
Singing what shameful things are done
Between the sunlit sea and the sun
　　When the land is left behind.

Book II
The Gathering of the Chiefs

Up over windy wastes and up
  Went Alfred over the shaws,
Shaken of the joy of giants,
  The joy without a cause.

In the slopes away to the western bays,   5
  Where blows not ever a tree,
He washed his soul in the west wind
  And his body in the sea.

And he set to rhyme his ale-measures,   9
  And he sang aloud his laws,
Because of the joy of the giants,
  The joy without a cause.

The King went gathering Wessex men,   13
  As grain out of the chaff;
The few that were alive to die,
Laughing, as littered skulls that lie
After lost battles turn to the sky
  An everlasting laugh.

The King went gathering Christian men,   19
  As wheat out of the husk;
Eldred, the Franklin by the sea,
And Mark, the man from Italy,
And Golan of the Sacred Tree,
  From the old tribe on Usk.

The rook croaked homeward heavily,   25
    The west was clear and warm,
The smoke of evening food and ease
Rose like a blue tree in the trees
    When he came to Eldred's farm.

But Eldred's farm was fallen awry,   30
    Like an old cripple's bones,
And Eldred's tools were red with rust,
And on his well was a green crust,
And purple thistles upward thrust,
    Between the kitchen stones.

But smoke of some good feasting   36
    Went upwards evermore,
And Eldred's doors stood wide apart
For loitering foot or labouring cart,
And Eldred's great and foolish heart
    Stood open like his door.

A mighty man was Eldred,   42
    A bulk for casks to fill,
His face a dreaming furnace,
    His body a walking hill.

In the old wars of Wessex   46
    His sword had sunken deep,
But all his friends, he sighed and said,
Were broken about Ethelred;
And between the deep drink and the dead

He had fallen upon sleep.

"Come not to me, King Alfred,   52
   Save always for the ale;
Why should my harmless hinds be slain
Because the chiefs cry once again,
As in all fights, that we shall gain,
   And in all fights we fail?

"Your scalds still thunder and prophesy   58
   That crown that never comes;
Friend, I will watch the certain things,
Swine, and slow moons like silver rings,
   And the ripening of the plums."

And Alfred answered, drinking,   63
   And gravely, without blame,
"Nor bear I boast of scald or king,
The thing I bear is a lesser thing,
   But comes in a better name.

"Out of the mouth of the Mother of God,   68
   More than the doors of doom,
I call the muster of Wessex men;
From grassy hamlet or ditch or den,
To break and be broken, God knows when,
   But I have seen for whom.

Out of the mouth of the Mother of God   74
   Like a little word come I;
For I go gathering Christian men

G. K. Chesterton's Early Poetry

From sunken paving and ford and fen,
To die in a battle, God knows when,
  By God, but I know why.

"And this is the word of Mary,   80
  The word of the world's desire:
'No more of comfort shall ye get,
Save that the sky grows darker yet
  And the sea rises higher.'"

Then silence sank. And slowly   85
  Arose the sea-land lord,
Like some vast beast for mystery,
He filled the room and porch and sky,
And from a cobwebbed nail on high
  Unhooked his heavy sword.

Up on the shrill sea-downs and up   91
  Went Alfred all alone,
And turned but once e'er the door was shut,
Shouting to Eldred over his butt,
That he bring all spears to the woodman's hut
  Hewn under Egbert's Stone.

And he turned his back and broke the fern   97
  And fought the moths of dusk,
And went on his way for other friends,
Friends fallen of all the wide world's ends,
From Rome that wrath and pardon sends
  And the grey tribes on Usk.

He saw gigantic tracks of death 103
  And many a shape of doom,
Good steadings to grey ashes gone
And a monk's house, white like a skeleton
  In the green crypt of the combe.

And in many a Roman villa 108
  Earth and her ivies eat,
Saw coloured pavements sink and fade
In flowers, and the windy colonnade
  Like the spectre of a street.

But the cold stars clustered 113
  Among the cold pines
Ere he was half on his pilgrimage
  Over the western lines.

And the white dawn widened 117
  Ere he came to the last pine,
Where Mark, the man from Italy,
  Still made the Christian sign.

The long farm lay on the large hill-side, 121
  Flat like a painted plan,
And by the side the low white house,
  Where dwelt the southland man.

A bronzed man, with a bird's bright eye, 125
  And a strong bird's beak and brow,
His skin was brown like buried gold,
And of certain of his sires was told

That they came in the shining ship of old,
   With Cæsar in the prow.

His fruit trees stood like soldiers,   131
   Drilled in a straight line,
His strange stiff olives did not fail,
And all the kings of the earth drank ale,
   But he drank wine.

Wide over wasted British plains   136
   Stood never an arch or dome,
Only the trees to toss and reel,
The tribes to bicker, the beasts to squeal;
But the eyes in his head were strong like steel,
   And his soul remembered Rome.

Then Alfred of the lonely spear   142
   Lifted his lion head;
And fronted with the Italian's eye
Asking him of his whence and why,
   King Alfred stood and said:

"I am that oft-defeated King   147
   Whose failure fills the land,
Who fled before the Danes of old,
Who chaffered with the Danes with gold,
Who now upon the Wessex wold
   Hardly has feet to stand.

"But out of the mouth of the Mother of God   153
   I have seen the truth like fire,

This—that the sky grows darker yet
  And the sea rises higher."

Long looked the Roman on the land;   157
  The trees as golden crowns
Blazed, drenched with dawn and dew-empearled,
While faintlier coloured, freshlier curled,
The clouds from underneath the world
  Stood up over the downs.

"These vines be ropes that drag me hard,"   163
  He said. "I go not far;
Where would you meet? For you must hold
Half Wiltshire and the White Horse wold,
And the Thames bank to Owsenfold,
  If Wessex goes to war.

"Guthrum sits strong on either bank   169
  And you must press his lines
Inwards, and eastward drive him down;
I doubt if you shall take the crown
Till you have taken London town.
  For me, I have the vines."

"If each man on the Judgment Day   175
  Meet God on a plain alone,"
Said Alfred, "I will speak for you
As for myself, and call it true
That you brought all fighting folk you knew
  Lined under Egbert's Stone.

"Though I be in the dust ere then,   181
   I know where you will be."
And shouldering suddenly his spear
He faded like some elfin fear,
Where the tall pines ran up, tier on tier
   Tree overtoppling tree.

He shouldered his spear at morning   187
   And laughed to lay it on,
But he leaned on his spear as on a staff,
With might and little mood to laugh,
Or ever he sighted chick or calf
   Of Colan of Caerleon.

For the man dwelt in a lost land   193
   Of boulders and broken men,
In a great grey cave far off to the south
Where a thick green forest stopped the mouth,
   Giving darkness in his den.

And the man was come like a shadow,   198
   From the shadow of Druid trees,
Where Usk, with mighty murmurings,
Past Caerleon of the fallen kings,
   Goes out to ghostly seas.

Last of a race in ruin—   203
   He spoke the speech of the Gaels;
His kin were in holy Ireland,
   Or up in the crags of Wales.

But his soul stood with his mother's folk,   207
  That were of the rain-wrapped isle,
Where Patrick and Brandan westerly
Looked out at last on a landless sea
  And the sun's last smile.

His harp was carved and cunning,   212
  As the Celtic craftsman makes,
Graven all over with twisting shapes
  Like many headless snakes.

His harp was carved and cunning,   216
  His sword prompt and sharp,
And he was gay when he held the sword,
  Sad when he held the harp.

For the great Gaels of Ireland   220
  Are the men that God made mad,
For all their wars are merry,
  And all their songs are sad.

He kept the Roman order,   224
  He made the Christian sign;
But his eyes grew often blind and bright,
And the sea that rose in the rocks at night
  Rose to his head like wine.

He made the sign of the cross of God,   229
  He knew the Roman prayer,
But he had unreason in his heart
  Because of the gods that were.

Even they that walked on the high cliffs, 233
   High as the clouds were then,
Gods of unbearable beauty
   That broke the hearts of men.

And whether in seat or saddle, 237
   Whether with frown or smile,
Whether at feast or fight was he,
He heard the noise of a nameless sea
   On an undiscovered isle.

Lifting the great green ivy 242
   And the great spear lowering,
One said, "I am Alfred of Wessex,
   And I am a conquered king."

And the man of the cave made answer, 246
   And his eyes were stars of scorn,
"And better kings were conquered
   Or ever your sires were born.

"What goddess was your mother, 250
   What fay your breed begot,
That you should not die with Uther
   And Arthur and Lancelot?

"But when you win you brag and blow, 254
   And when you lose you rail,
Army of eastland yokels
   Not strong enough to fail."

"I bring not boast or railing,"   258
   Spake Alfred not in ire,
"I bring of Our Lady a lesson set,
This—that the sky grows darker yet
   And the sea rises higher."

Then Colan of the Sacred Tree   263
   Tossed his black mane on high,
And cried, as rigidly he rose,
"And if the sea and sky be foes,
   We will tame the sea and sky."

Smiled Alfred, "Seek ye a fable   268
   More dizzy and more dread
Than all your mad barbarian tales,
   Where the sky stands on its head?

"A tale where a man looks down on the sky   272
   That has long looked down on him;
A tale where a man can swallow a sea
   That might swallow the seraphim.

"Bring to the hut by Egbert's Stone   276
   All bills and bows ye have."
And Alfred strode off rapidly,
And Colan of the Sacred Tree
   Went slowly to his cave.

Book III
The Harp of Alfred

In a tree that yawned and twisted
  The King's few goods were flung,
A mass-book mildewed, line by line,
And weapons and a skin of wine,
  And an old harp unstrung.

By the yawning tree in the twilight
  The King unbound his sword,
Severed the harp of all his goods,
And there in the cool and soundless woods
  Sounded a single chord.

Then laughed; and watched the finches flash,
  The sullen flies in swarm,
And went unarmed over the hills,
  With the harp upon his arm,

Until he came to the White Horse Vale
  And saw across the plains,
In the twilight high and far and fell,
Like the fiery terraces of hell,
  The camp fires of the Danes—

The fires of the Great Army
  That was made of iron men,
Whose lights of sacrilege and scorn
Ran around England red as morn,
Fires over Glastonbury Thorn—

Fires out on Ely Fen.

And as he went by White Horse Vale 26
   He saw lie wan and wide
The old horse graven, God knows when,
By gods or beasts or what things then
Walked a new world instead of men
   And scrawled on the hill-side.

And when he came to White Horse Down 32
   The great White Horse was grey,
For it was ill scoured of the weed,
And lichen and thorn could crawl and feed,
Since the foes of settled house and creed
   Had swept old works away.

King Alfred gazed all sorrowful 38
   At thistle and mosses grey,
Till a rally of Danes with shield and bill
Rolled drunk over the dome of the hill,
And hearing of his harp and skill,
   They dragged him to their play.

And as they went through the high green grass 44
   They roared like the great green sea;
But when they came to the red camp fire
   They were silent suddenly.

And as they went up the wastes away 48
   They went reeling to and fro;
But when they came to the red camp fire

They stood all in a row.

For golden in the firelight,   52
  With a smile carved on his lips,
And a beard curled right cunningly,
Was Guthrum of the Northern Sea,
  The emperor of the ships—

With three great earls King Guthrum   57
  Went the rounds from fire to fire,
With Harold, nephew of the King,
And Ogier of the Stone and Sling,
And Elf, whose gold lute had a string
  That sighed like all desire.

The Earls of the Great Army   63
  That no men born could tire,
Whose flames anear him or aloof
Took hold of towers or walls of proof,
Fire over Glastonbury roof
  And out on Ely, fire.

And Guthrum heard the soldiers' tale   69
  And bade the stranger play;
Not harshly, but as one on high,
On a marble pillar in the sky,
Who sees all folk that live and die—
  Pigmy and far away.

And Alfred, King of Wessex,   75
  Looked on his conqueror—

And his hands hardened; but he played,
And leaving all later hates unsaid,
He sang of some old British raid
　　On the wild west march of yore.

He sang of war in the warm wet shires, 81
　　Where rain nor fruitage fails,
Where England of the motley states
Deepens like a garden to the gates
　　In the purple walls of Wales.

He sang of the seas of savage heads 86
　　And the seas and seas of spears,
Boiling all over Offa's Dyke,
What time a Wessex club could strike
　　The kings of the mountaineers.

Till Harold laughed and snatched the harp, 91
　　The kinsman of the King,
A big youth, beardless like a child,
Whom the new wine of war sent wild,
　　Smote, and began to sing—

And he cried of the ships as eagles 96
　　That circle fiercely and fly,
And sweep the seas and strike the towns
　　From Cyprus round to Skye.

How swiftly and with peril 100
　　They gather all good things,
The high horns of the forest beasts,

Or the secret stones of Kings.

"For Rome was given to rule the world,   104
  And gat of it little joy—
But we, but we shall enjoy the world,
  The whole huge world a toy.

"Great wine like blood from Burgundy,   108
  Cloaks like the clouds from Tyre,
And marble like solid moonlight,
  And gold like frozen fire.

"Smells that a man might swill in a cup,   112
  Stones that a man might eat,
And the great smooth women like ivory
  That the Turks sell in the street."

He sang the song of the thief of the world,   116
  And the gods that love the thief;
And he yelled aloud at the cloister-yards,
  Where men go gathering grief.

"Well have you sung, O stranger,   120
  Of death on the dyke in Wales,
Your chief was a bracelet-giver;
But the red unbroken river
Of a race runs not for ever,
  But suddenly it fails.

"Doubtless your sires were sword-swingers   126
  When they waded fresh from foam,
Before they were turned to women

By the god of the nails from Rome;

"But since you bent to the shaven men,   134
   Who neither lust nor smite,
Thunder of Thor, we hunt you,
   A hare on the mountain height."

King Guthrum smiled a little,   134
   And said, "It is enough,
Nephew, let Elf retune the string;
A boy must needs like bellowing,
But the old ears of a careful king
   Are glad of songs less rough."

Blue-eyed was Elf the minstrel,   140
   With womanish hair and ring,
Yet heavy was his hand on sword
   Though light upon the string.

And as he stirred the strings of the harp   144
   To notes but four or five,
The heart of each man moved in him
   Like a babe buried alive.

And they felt the land of the folk-songs   148
   Spread southward of the Dane,
And they heard the good Rhine flowing
   In the heart of all Allemagne.

They felt the land of the folk-songs,   152
   Where the gifts hang on the tree,
Where the girls give ale at morning

And the tears come easily.

The mighty people, womanlike, 156
   That have pleasure in their pain
As he sang of Balder beautiful,
   Whom the heavens loved in vain.

As he sang of Balder beautiful, 160
   Whom the heavens could not save,
Till the world was like a sea of tears
   And every soul a wave.

"There is always a thing forgotten 164
   When all the world goes well;
A thing forgotten, as long ago
When the gods forgot the mistlètoe,
And soundless as an arrow of snow
   The arrow of anguish fell.

"The thing on the blind side of the heart, 170
   On the wrong side of the door,
The green plant groweth, menacing
Almighty lovers in the spring;
There is always a forgotten thing,
   And love is not secure."

And all that sat by the fire were sad, 176
   Save Ogier, who was stern,
And his eyes hardened even to stones,
   As he took the harp in turn;

Earl Ogier of the Stone and Sling   *180*
    Was odd to ear and sight,
Old he was, but his locks were red,
And jests were all the words he said
Yet he was sad at board and bed
    And savage in the fight.

"You sing of the young gods easily   *186*
    In the days when you are young;
But I go smelling yew and sods,
And I know there are gods behind the gods,
    Gods that are best unsung.

"And a man grows ugly for women,   *191*
    And a man grows dull with ale,
Well if he find in his soul at last
    Fury, that does not fail.

"The wrath of the gods behind the gods   *195*
    Who would rend all gods and men,
Well if the old man's heart hath still
Wheels sped of rage and roaring will,
Like cataracts to break down and kill,
    Well for the old man then—

"While there is one tall shrine to shake,   *201*
    Or one live man to rend;
For the wrath of the gods behind the gods
    Who are weary to make an end.

"There lives one moment for a man   205
   When the door at his shoulder shakes,
When the taut rope parts under the pull,
And the barest branch is beautiful
   One moment, while it breaks.

"So rides my soul upon the sea   210
   That drinks the howling ships,
Though in black jest it bows and nods
Under the moons with silver rods,
I know it is roaring at the gods,
   Waiting the last eclipse.

"And in the last eclipse the sea   216
   Shall stand up like a tower,
Above all moons made dark and riven,
Hold up its foaming head in heaven,
   And laugh, knowing its hour.

"And the high ones in the happy town   221
   Propped of the planets seven,
Shall know a new light in the mind,
A noise about them and behind,
Shall hear an awful voice, and find
   Foam in the courts of heaven.

"And you that sit by the fire are young,   227
   And true loves wait for you;
But the king and I grow old, grow old,
   And hate alone is true."

And Guthrum shook his head but smiled,　　　231
　　For he was a mighty clerk,
And had read lines in the Latin books,
　　When all the north was dark.

He said, "I am older than you, Ogier;　　　235
　　Not all things would I rend,
For whether life be bad or good,
　　It is best to abide the end."

He took the great harp wearily,　　　239
　　Even Guthrum of the Danes,
With wide eyes bright as the one long day
　　On the long polar plains.

For he sang of a wheel returning,　　　243
　　And the mire trod back to mire,
And how red hells and golden heavens
　　Are castles in the fire.

"It is good to sit where the good tales go,　　　247
　　To sit as our fathers sat;
But the hour shall come after his youth,
When a man shall know not tales but truth,
　　And his heart fail thereat.

"When he shall read what is written　　　252
　　So plain in clouds and clods,
When he shall hunger without hope
　　Even for evil gods.

"For this is a heavy matter,
   And the truth is cold to tell;
Do we not know, have we not heard,
The soul is like a lost bird,
   The body a broken shell.

256

"And a man hopes, being ignorant
   Till in white woods apart
He finds at last the lost bird dead:
And a man may still lift up his head
   But never more his heart.

261

"There comes no noise but weeping
   Out of the ancient sky,
And a tear is in the tiniest flower
   Because the gods must die.

266

"The little brooks are very sweet,
   Like a girl's ribbons curled,
But the great sea is bitter
   That washes all the world.

270

"Strong are the Roman roses,
   Or the free flowers of the heath,
But every flower, like a flower of the sea,
   Smelleth with the salt of death.

274

"And the heart of the locked battle
   Is the happiest place for men;
When shrieking souls as shafts go by
And many have died and all may die;

278

Though this word be a mystery,
    Death is most distant then.

"Death blazes bright above the cup,   284
    And clear above the crown;
But in that dream of battle
    We seem to tread it down.

"Wherefore I am a great king,   288
    And waste the world in vain,
Because man hath not other power,
Save that in dealing death for dower,
He may forget it for an hour
    To remember it again."

And slowly his hands and thoughtfully   294
    Fell from the lifted lyre,
And the owls moaned from the mighty trees
Till Alfred caught it to his knees
    And smote it as in ire.

He heaved the head of the harp on high   299
    And swept the framework barred,
And his stroke had all the rattle and spark
    Of horses flying hard.

"When God put man in a garden   303
    He girt him with a sword,
And sent him forth a free knight
    That might betray his lord;

"He brake Him and betrayed Him, 307
   And fast and far he fell,
Till you and I may stretch our necks
   And burn our beards in hell.

"But though I lie on the floor of the world, 311
   With the seven sins for rods,
I would rather fall with Adam
   Than rise with all your gods.

"What have the strong gods given? 315
   Where have the glad gods led?
When Guthrum sits on a hero's throne
   And asks if he is dead?

"Sirs, I am but a nameless man, 319
   A rhymester without home,
Yet since I come of the Wessex clay
   And carry the cross of Rome,

"I will even answer the mighty earl 323
   That asked of Wessex men
Why they be meek and monkish folk,
And bow to the White Lord's broken yoke;
What sign have we save blood and smoke?
   Here is my answer then.

"That on you is fallen the shadow, 329
   And not upon the Name;
That though we scatter and though we fly,
And you hang over us like the sky,

You are more tired of victory,
   Than we are tired of shame.

"That though you hunt the Christian man   335
   Like a hare on the hill-side,
The hare has still more heart to run
   Than you have heart to ride.

"That though all lances split on you,   339
   All swords be heaved in vain,
We have more lust again to lose
   Than you to win again.

"Your lord sits high in the saddle,   343
   A broken-hearted king,
But our king Alfred, lost from fame,
Fallen among foes or bonds of shame,
In I know not what mean trade or name,
   Has still some song to sing;

"Our monks go robed in rain and snow,   349
   But the heart of flame therein,
But you go clothed in feasts and flames,
   When all is ice within;

"Nor shall all iron dooms make dumb   353
   Men wondering ceaselessly,
If it be not better to fast for joy
   Than feast for misery.

"Nor monkish order only   357
   Slides down, as field to fen,

All things achieved and chosen pass,
As the White Horse fades in the grass,
   No work of Christian men.

"Ere the sad gods that made your gods 362
   Saw their sad sunrise pass,
The White Horse of the White Horse Vale,
That you have left to darken and fail,
   Was cut out of the grass.

"Therefore your end is on you, 367
   Is on you and your kings,
Not for a fire in Ely fen,
Not that your gods are nine or ten,
But because it is only Christian men
   Guard even heathen things.

"For our God hath blessed creation, 373
   Calling it good. I know
What spirit with whom you blindly band
Hath blessed destruction with his hand;
Yet by God's death the stars shall stand
   And the small apples grow."

And the King, with harp on shoulder, 379
   Stood up and ceased his song;
And the owls moaned from the mighty trees,
   And the Danes laughed loud and long.

Book IV
The Woman in the Forest

Thick thunder of the snorting swine,
   Enormous in the gloam,
Rending among all roots that cling,
And the wild horses whinnying,
Were the night's noises when the King
   Shouldering his harp, went home.

With eyes of owl and feet of fox,   7
   Full of all thoughts he went;
He marked the tilt of the pagan camp,
The paling of pine, the sentries' tramp,
And the one great stolen altar-lamp
   Over Guthrum in his tent.

By scrub and thorn in Ethandune   13
   That night the foe had lain;
Whence ran across the heather grey
The old stones of a Roman way;
And in a wood not far away
   The pale road split in twain.

He marked the wood and the cloven ways   19
   With an old captain's eyes,
And he thought how many a time had he
Sought to see Doom he could not see;
How ruin had come and victory,
   And both were a surprise.

Even so he had watched and wondered
   Under Ashdown from the plains;
With Ethelred praying in his tent,
Till the white hawthorn swung and bent,
As Alfred rushed his spears and rent
   The shield-wall of the Danes.

                                          25

Even so he had watched and wondered,
   Knowing neither less nor more,
Till all his lords lay dying,
And axes on axes plying,
Flung him, and drove him flying
   Like a pirate to the shore.

                                          31

Wise he had been before defeat,
   And wise before success;
Wise in both hours and ignorant,
   Knowing neither more nor less.

                                          37

As he went down to the river-hut
   He knew a night-shade scent,
Owls did as evil cherubs rise,
With little wings and lantern eyes,
As though he sank through the under-skies;
   But down and down he went.

                                          41

As he went down to the river-hut
   He went as one that fell;
Seeing the high forest domes and spars.
Dim green or torn with golden scars,
As the proud look up at the evil stars,

                                          47

In the red heavens of hell.

For he must meet by the river-hut   53
  Them he had bidden to arm,
Mark from the towers of Italy,
And Colan of the Sacred Tree,
And Eldred who beside the sea
  Held heavily his farm.

The roof leaned gaping to the grass,   59
  As a monstrous mushroom lies;
Echoing and empty seemed the place;
But opened in a little space
A great grey woman with scarred face
  And strong and humbled eyes.

King Alfred was but a meagre man,   65
  Bright eyed, but lean and pale:
And swordless, with his harp and rags,
He seemed a beggar, such as lags
  Looking for crusts and ale.

And the woman, with a woman's eyes   70
  Of pity at once and ire,
Said, when that she had glared a span,
"There is a cake for any man
  If he will watch the fire."

And Alfred, bowing heavily,   75
  Sat down the fire to stir,
And even as the woman pitied him

So did he pity her.

Saying, "O great heart in the night,   79
      O best cast forth for worst,
Twilight shall melt and morning stir,
And no kind thing shall come to her,
Till God shall turn the world over
      And all the last are first.

"And well may God with the serving-folk   85
      Cast in His dreadful lot;
Is not He too a servant,
      And is not He forgot?

"For was not God my gardener   89
      And silent like a slave;
That opened oaks on the uplands
      Or thicket in graveyard gave?

"And was not God my armourer,   93
      All patient and unpaid,
That sealed my skull as a helmet,
      And ribs for hauberk made?

"Did not a great grey servant   97
      Of all my sires and me,
Build this pavilion of the pines,
And herd the fowls and fill the vines,
And labour and pass and leave no signs
      Save mercy and mystery?

"For God is a great servant,
    And rose before the day,
From some primordial slumber torn;
But all we living later born
Sleep on, and rise after the morn,
    And the Lord has gone away.   103

"On things half sprung from sleeping,
    All sleepy suns have shone,
They stretch stiff arms, the yawning trees,
The beasts blink upon hands and knees,
Man is awake and does and sees—
    But Heaven has done and gone.   109

For who shall guess the good riddle
    Or speak of the Holiest,
Save in faint figures and failing words,
Who loves, yet laughs among the swords,
    Labours, and is at rest?   115

"But some see God like Guthrum,
    Crowned, with a great beard curled,
But I see God like a good giant,
    That, labouring, lifts the world.   120

"Wherefore was God in Golgotha,
    Slain as a serf is slain;
And hate He had of prince and peer,
And love He had and made good cheer,
Of them that, like this woman here,
    Go powerfully in pain.   124

"But in this grey morn of man's life, 130
   Cometh sometime to the mind
A little light that leaps and flies,
   Like a star blown on the wind.

"A star of nowhere, a nameless star, 134
   A light that spins and swirls,
And cries that even in hedge and hill,
Even on earth, it may go ill
   At last with the evil earls.

"A dancing sparkle, a doubtful star, 139
   On the waste wind whirled and driven;
But it seems to sing of a wilder worth,
A time discrowned of doom and birth,
And the kingdom of the poor on earth
   Come, as it is in heaven.

"But even though such days endure, 145
   How shall it profit her?
Who shall go groaning to the grave,
With many a meek and mighty slave,
Field-breaker and fisher on the wave,
   And woodman and waggoner.

"Bake ye the big world all again 151
   A cake with kinder leaven;
Yet these are sorry evermore—
Unless there be a little door,
   A little door in heaven."

And as he wept for the woman   156
    He let her business be,
And like his royal oath and rash
The good food fell upon the ash
    And blackened instantly.

Screaming, the woman caught a cake   161
    Yet burning from the bar,
And struck him suddenly on the face,
    Leaving a scarlet scar.

King Alfred stood up wordless,   165
    A man dead with surprise,
And torture stood and the evil things
That are in the childish hearts of kings
    An instant in his eyes.

And even as he stood and stared   170
    Drew round him in the dusk
Those friends creeping from far-off farms,
Marcus with all his slaves in arms,
And the strange spears hung with ancient charms
    Of Colan of the Usk.

With one whole farm marching afoot   176
    The trampled road resounds,
Farm-hands and farm-beasts blundering by
And jars of mead and stores of rye,
Where Eldred strode above his high
    And thunder-throated hounds.

And grey cattle and silver lowed
   Against the unlifted morn,
And straw clung to the spear-shafts tall.
And a boy went before them all
   Blowing a ram's horn.

182

As mocking such rude revelry,
   The dim clan of the Gael
Came like a bad king's burial-end,
With dismal robes that drop and rend
   And demon pipes that wail—

187

In long, outlandish garments,
   Torn, though of antique worth,
With Druid beards and Druid spears,
As a resurrected race appears
   Out of an elder earth.

192

And though the King had called them forth
   And knew them for his own,
So still each eye stood like a gem,
So spectral hung each broidered hem,
Grey carven men he fancied them,
   Hewn in an age of stone.

197

And the two wild peoples of the north
   Stood fronting in the gloam,
And heard and knew each in its mind
The third great thunder on the wind,
The living walls that hedge mankind,
   The walking walls of Rome.

203

The Ballad of the White Horse

Mark's were the mixed tribes of the west,   *209*
  Of many a hue and strain,
Gurth, with rank hair like yellow grass,
And the Cornish fisher, Gorlias,
And Halmer, come from his first mass,
  Lately baptized, a Dane.

But like one man in armour   *215*
  Those hundreds trod the field,
From red Arabia to the Tyne
The earth had heard that marching-line,
Since the cry on the hill Capitoline,
  And the fall of the golden shield.

And the earth shook and the King stood still   *221*
  Under the greenwood bough,
And the smoking cake lay at his feet
  And the blow was on his brow.

Then Alfred laughed out suddenly,   *225*
  Like thunder in the spring,
Till shook aloud the lintel-beams,
And the squirrels stirred in dusty dreams,
And the startled birds went up in streams,
  For the laughter of the King.

And the beasts of the earth and the birds looked
    down,   *231*
  In a wild solemnity,
On a stranger sight than a sylph or elf,

On one man laughing at himself
   Under the greenwood tree—

The giant laughter of Christian men   236
   That roars through a thousand tales,
Where greed is an ape and pride is an ass,
And Jack's away with his master's lass,
And the miser is banged with all his brass,
   The farmer with all his flails;

Tales that tumble and tales that trick,   242
   Yet end not all in scorning—
Of kings and clowns in a merry plight,
And the clock gone wrong and the world gone right,
That the mummers sing upon Christmas night
   And Christmas Day in the morning.

"Now here is a good warrant,"   248
   Cried Alfred, "by my sword;
For he that is struck for an ill servant
   Should be a kind lord.

"He that has been a servant   252
   Knows more than priests and kings,
But he that has been an ill servant,
   He knows all earthly things.

"Pride flings frail palaces at the sky,   256
   As a man flings up sand,
But the firm feet of humility
   Take hold of heavy land.

"Pride juggles with her toppling towers,   260
    They strike the sun and cease,
But the firm feet of humility
    They grip the ground like trees.

"He that hath failed in a little thing   264
    Hath a sign upon the brow;
And the Earls of the Great Army
    Have no such seal to show.

"The red print on my forehead,   268
    Small flame for a red star,
In the van of the violent marching, then
When the sky is torn of the trumpets ten,
And the hands of the happy howling men
    Fling wide the gates of war.

"This blow that I return not   274
    Ten times will I return
On kings and earls of all degree,
And armies wide as empires be
Shall slide like landslips to the sea
    If the red star burn.

"One man shall drive a hundred,   280
    As the dead kings drave;
Before me rocking hosts be riven,
And battering cohorts backwards driven,
For I am the first king known of Heaven
    That has been struck like a slave.

"Up on the old white road, brothers,   286
    Up on the Roman walls!
For this is the night of the drawing of swords,
And the tainted tower of the heathen hordes
Leans to our hammers, fires and cords,
    Leans a little and falls.

"Follow the star that lives and leaps,   292
    Follow the sword that sings,
For we go gathering heathen men,
A terrible harvest, ten by ten,
As the wrath of the last red autumn—then
    When Christ reaps down the kings.

"Follow a light that leaps and spins,   298
    Follow the fire unfurled!
For riseth up against realm and rod,
A thing forgotten, a thing downtrod,
The last lost giant, even God,
    Is risen against the world."

Roaring they went o'er the Roman wall,   304
    And roaring up the lane,
Their torches tossed a ladder of fire,
Higher their hymn was heard and higher,
More sweet for hate and for heart's desire,
And up in the northern scrub and brier,
    They fell upon the Dane.

BOOK V
ETHADUNE: THE FIRST STROKE

King Guthrum was a dread king,
   Like death out of the north;
Shrines without name or number
He rent and rolled as lumber,
From Chester to the Humber
   He drove his foemen forth.

The Roman villas heard him   7
   In the valley of the Thames,
Come over the hills roaring
Above their roofs, and pouring
On spire and stair and flooring
   Brimstone and pitch and flames.

Sheer o'er the great chalk uplands   13
   And the hill of the Horse went he,
Till high on Hampshire beacons
   He saw the southern sea.

High on the heights of Wessex   17
   He saw the southern brine,
And turned him to a conquered land,
And where the northern thornwoods stand,
And the road parts on either hand,
   There came to him a sign.

King Guthrum was a war-chief,   23
   A wise man in the field,

And though he prospered well, and knew
How Alfred's folk were sad and few,
Not less with weighty care he drew
    Long lines for pike and shield.

King Guthrum lay on the upper land,   29
    On a single road at gaze,
And his foe must come with lean array,
Up the left arm of the cloven way,
    To the meeting of the ways.

And long ere the noise of armour,   34
    An hour ere the break of light,
The woods awoke with crash and cry,
And the birds sprang clamouring harsh and high,
And the rabbits ran like an elves' army
    Ere Alfred came in sight.

The live wood came at Guthrum,   40
    On foot and claw and wing,
The nests were noisy overhead,
For Alfred and the star of red,
All life went forth, and the forest fled
    Before the face of the King.

But halted in the woodways   46
    Christ's few were grim and grey,
And each with a small, far, bird-like sight
Saw the high folly of the fight;
And though strange joys had grown in the night,
    Despair grew with the day.

And when white dawn crawled through the wood,   52
  Like cold foam of a flood,
Then weakened every warrior's mood,
In hope, though not in hardihood;
And each man sorrowed as he stood
  In the fashion of his blood.

For the Saxon Franklin sorrowed   58
  For the things that had been fair;
For the dear dead woman, crimson-clad,
And the great feasts and the friends he had;
But the Celtic prince's soul was sad
  For the things that never were.

In the eyes Italian all things   64
  But a black laughter died;
And Alfred flung his shield to earth
  And smote his breast and cried—

"I wronged a man to his slaying,   68
  And a woman to her shame,
And once I looked on a sworn maid
  That was wed to the Holy Name.

"And once I took my neighbour's wife,   72
  That was bound to an eastland man,
In the starkness of my evil youth,
  Before my griefs began.

"People, if you have any prayers,   76
  Say prayers for me:

And lay me under a Christian stone
In that lost land I thought my own,
To wait till the holy horn is blown,
  And all poor men are free."

Then Eldred of the idle farm
  Leaned on his ancient sword,
As fell his heavy words and few;
And his eyes were of such alien blue
As gleams where the Northman saileth new
  Into an unknown fiord.

82

"I was a fool and wasted ale—
  My slaves found it sweet;
I was a fool and wasted bread,
  And the birds had bread to eat.

88

"The kings go up and the kings go down,
  And who knows who shall rule;
Next night a king may starve or sleep,
But men and birds and beasts shall weep
  At the burial of a fool.

92

"O, drunkards in my cellar,
  Boys in my apple tree,
The world grows stern and strange and new,
And wise men shall govern you,
  And you shall weep for me.

97

"But yoke me my own oxen,
  Down to my own farm;

102

My own dog will whine for me,
My own friends will bend the knee,
And the foes I slew openly
    Have never wished me harm."

And all were moved a little,   108
    But Colan stood apart,
Having first pity, and after
Hearing, like rat in rafter,
That little worm of laughter
    That eats the Irish heart.

And his grey-green eyes were cruel,   114
    And the smile of his mouth waxed hard,
And he said, "And when did Britain
    Become your burying-yard?

"Before the Romans lit the land,   118
    When schools and monks were none,
We reared such stones to the sun-god
    As might put out the sun.

"The tall trees of Britain   122
    We worshipped and were wise,
But you shall raid the whole land through
And never a tree shall talk to you,
Though every leaf is a tongue taught true
    And the forest is full of eyes.

"On one round hill to the seaward   128
    The trees grow tall and grey

And the trees talk together
  When all men are away.

"O'er a few round hills forgotten   132
  The trees grow tall in rings,
And the trees talk together
  Of many pagan things.

"Yet I could lie and listen   136
  With a cross upon my clay,
And hear unhurt for ever
  What the trees of Britain say."

A proud man was the Roman,   140
  His speech a single one,
But his eyes were like an eagle's eyes
  That is staring at the sun.

"Dig for me where I die," he said,   144
  "If first or last I fall—
Dead on the fell at the first charge,
  Or dead by Wantage wall;

"Lift not my head from bloody ground,   148
  Bear not my body home,
For all the earth is Roman earth
  And I shall die in Rome."

Then Alfred, King of England,   152
  Bade blow the horns of war,
And fling the Golden Dragon out,
With crackle and acclaim and shout,

Scrolled and aflame and far.

And under the Golden Dragon 157
    Went Wessex all along,
Past the sharp point of the cloven ways,
Out from the black wood into the blaze
    Of sun and steel and song.

And when they came to the open land 162
    They wheeled, deployed and stood;
Midmost were Marcus and the King,
And Eldred on the right-hand wing,
And leftwards Colan darkling,
    In the last shade of the wood.

But the Earls of the Great Army 168
    Lay like a long half moon,
Ten poles before their palisades,
With wide-winged helms and runic blades
Red giants of an age of raids,
    In the thornland of Ethandune.

Midmost the saddles rose and swayed, 174
    And a stir of horses' manes,
Where Guthrum and a few rode high
On horses seized in victory;
But Ogier went on foot to die,
    In the old way of the Danes.

Far to the King's left Elf the bard 180
    Led on the eastern wing

With songs and spells that change the blood;
And on the King's right Harold stood,
  The kinsman of the King.

Young Harold, coarse, with colours gay,   185
  Smoking with oil and musk,
And the pleasant violence of the young,
Pushed through his people, giving tongue
Foewards, where, grey as cobwebs hung,
  The banners of the Usk.

But as he came before his line   191
  A little space along,
His beardless face broke into mirth,
And he cried: "What broken bits of earth
Are here? For what their clothes are worth
  I would sell them for a song."

For Colan was hung with raiment   197
  Tattered like autumn leaves,
And his men were all as thin as saints,
  And all as poor as thieves.

No bows nor slings nor bolts they bore,   201
  But bills and pikes ill-made;
And none but Colan bore a sword,
  And rusty was its blade.

And Colan's eyes with mystery   205
  And iron laughter stirred,
And he spoke aloud, but lightly,

Not labouring to be heard.

"Oh, truly we be broken hearts,   209
   For that cause, it is said,
We light our candles to that Lord
   That broke Himself for bread.

"But though we hold but bitterly   213
   What land the Saxon leaves,
Though Ireland be but a land of saints,
   And Wales a land of thieves,

"I say you yet shall weary   217
   Of the working of your word,
That stricken spirits never strike
   Nor lean hands hold a sword.

"And if ever ye ride in Ireland,   221
   The jest may yet be said,
There is the land of broken hearts,
   And the land of broken heads."

Not less barbarian laughter   225
   Choked Harold like a flood,
"And shall I fight with scarecrows
   That am of Guthrum's blood?

"Meeting may be of war-men,   229
   Where the best war-man wins;
But all this carrion a man shoots
   Before the fight begins."

And stopping in his onward strides, 233
   He snatched a bow in scorn
   From some mean slave, and bent it on
Colan, whose doom grew dark; and shone
Stars evil over Caerleon,
   In the place where he was born.

For Colan had not bow nor sling, 239
   On a lonely sword leaned he,
Like Arthur on Excalibur
   In the battle by the sea.

To his great gold ear-ring Harold 243
   Tugged back the feathered tail,
And swift had sprung the arrow,
   But swifter sprang the Gael.

Whirling the one sword round his head, 247
   A great wheel in the sun,
He sent it splendid through the sky,
Flying before the shaft could fly—
It smote Earl Harold over the eye,
   And blood began to run.

Colan stood bare and weaponless, 253
   Earl Harold, as in pain,
Strove for a smile, put hand to head,
Stumbled and suddenly fell dead;
And the small white daisies all waxed red
   With blood out of his brain.

And all at that marvel of the sword,   *259*
   Cast like a stone to slay,
Cried out. Said Alfred: "Who would see
Signs, must give all things. Verily
Man shall not taste of victory
   Till he throws his sword away."

Then Alfred, prince of England,   *265*
   And all the Christian earls,
Unhooked their swords and held them up,
Each offered to Colan, like a cup
   Of chrysolite and pearls.

And the King said, "Do thou take my sword   *270*
   Who have done this deed of fire,
For this is the manner of Christian men,
Whether of steel or priestly pen,
That they cast their hearts out of their ken
   To get their heart's desire.

"And whether ye swear a hive of monks,   *276*
   Or one fair wife to friend,
This is the manner of Christian men,
   That their oath endures the end.

"For love, our Lord, at the end of the world,   *280*
   Sits a red horse like a throne,
With a brazen helm and an iron bow,
   But one arrow alone.

"Love with the shield of the Broken Heart   284
   Ever his bow doth bend,
With a single shaft for a single prize,
And the ultimate bolt that parts and flies
Comes with a thunder of split skies,
   And a sound of souls that rend.

"So shall you earn a king's sword,   290
   Who cast your sword away."
And the King took, with a random eye,
A rude axe from a hind hard by
   And turned him to the fray.

For the swords of the Earls of Daneland   295
   Flamed round the fallen lord.
The first blood woke the trumpet-tune,
As in monk's rhyme or wizard's rune,
Beginneth the battle of Ethandune
   With the throwing of the sword.

Book VI
Ethandune: The Slaying of the Chiefs

As the sea flooding the flat sands
　　Flew on the sea-born horde,
The two hosts shocked with dust and din,
Left of the Latian paladin,
Clanged all Prince Harold's howling kin
　　On Colan and the sword.

Crashed in the midst on Marcus,   *7*
　　Ogier with Guthrum by,
And eastward of such central stir,
Far to the right and faintlier,
The house of Elf the harp-player,
　　Struck Eldred's with a cry.

The centre swat for weariness,   *13*
　　Stemming the screaming horde,
And wearily went Colan's hands
　　That swung King Alfred's sword.

But like a cloud of morning   *17*
　　To eastward easily,
Tall Eldred broke the sea of spears
　　As a tall ship breaks the sea.

His face like a sanguine sunset,   *21*
　　His shoulder a Wessex down,
His hand like a windy hammer-stroke;
Men could not count the crests he broke,

So fast the crests went down.

As the tall white devil of the Plague   *26*
   Moves out of Asian skies,
With his foot on a waste of cities
   And his head in a cloud of flies;

Or purple and peacock skies grow dark   *30*
   With a moving locust-tower;
Or tawny sand-winds tall and dry,
Like hell's red banners beat and fly,
When death comes out of Araby,
   Was Eldred in his hour.

But while he moved like a massacre   *36*
   He murmured as in sleep,
And his words were all of low hedges
   And little fields and sheep.

Even as he strode like a pestilence,   *40*
   That strides from Rhine to Rome,
He thought how tall his beans might be
   If ever he went home.

Spoke some stiff piece of childish prayer,   *44*
   Dull as the distant chimes,
That thanked our God for good eating
   And corn and quiet times—

Till on the helm of a high chief   *48*
   Fell shatteringly his brand,
And the helm broke and the bone broke

And the sword broke in his hand.

Then from the yelling Northmen 52
    Driven splintering on him ran
Full seven spears, and the seventh
    Was never made by man.

Seven spears, and the seventh 56
    Was wrought as the faerie blades,
And given to Elf the minstrel
    By the monstrous water-maids;

By them that dwell where luridly 60
    Lost waters of the Rhine
Move among roots of nations,
    Being sunken for a sign.

Under all graves they murmur, 64
    They murmur and rebel,
Down to the buried kingdoms creep,
And like a lost rain roar and weep
    O'er the red heavens of hell.

Thrice drowned was Elf the minstrel, 69
    And washed as dead on sand;
And the third time men found him
    The spear was in his hand.

Seven spears went about Eldred, 73
    Like stays about a mast;
But there was sorrow by the sea
    For the driving of the last.

Six spears thrust upon Eldred 77
  Were splintered while he laughed;
One spear thrust into Eldred,
  Three feet of blade and shaft.

And from the great heart grievously 81
  Came forth the shaft and blade,
And he stood with the face of a dead man,
  Stood a little, and swayed—

Then fell, as falls a battle-tower, 85
  On smashed and struggling spears.
Cast down from some unconquered town
That, rushing earthward, carries down
Loads of live men of all renown—
  Archers and engineers.

And a great clamour of Christian men 91
  Went up in agony,
Crying, "Fallen is the tower of Wessex
  That stood beside the sea."

Centre and right the Wessex guard 95
  Grew pale for doubt and fear,
And the flank failed at the advance,
For the death-light on the wizard lance—
  The star of the evil spear.

"Stand like an oak," cried Marcus, 100
  "Stand like a Roman wall!
Eldred the Good is fallen—

Are you too good to fall?

"When we were wan and bloodless   *104*
    He gave you ale enow;
The pirates deal with him as dung,
    God! are you bloodless now?"

"Grip, Wulf and Gorlias, grip the ash!   *108*
    Slaves, and I make you free!
Stamp, Hildred hard in English land,
Stand Gurth, stand Gorlias, Gawen stand!
Hold, Halfgar, with the other hand,
    Halmer, hold up on knee!

"The lamps are dying in your homes,   *114*
    The fruits upon your bough;
Even now your old thatch smoulders, Gurth,
Now is the judgment of the earth,
    Now is the death-grip, now!"

For thunder of the captain,   *119*
    Not less the Wessex line,
Leaned back and reeled a space to rear
As Elf charged with the Rhine maids' spear,
    And roaring like the Rhine.

For the men were borne by the waving walls   *124*
    Of woods and clouds that pass,
By dizzy plains and drifting sea,
And they mixed God with glamoury,
God with the gods of the burning tree

And the wizard's tower and glass.

But Mark was come of the glittering towns 130
  Where hot white details show,
  Where men can number and expound,
  And his faith grew in a hard ground
  Of doubt and reason and falsehood found,
  Where no faith else could grow.

Belief that grew of all beliefs 136
  One moment back was blown
And belief that stood on unbelief
  Stood up iron and alone.

The Wessex crescent backwards 140
  Crushed, as with bloody spear
Went Elf roaring and routing,
And Mark against Elf yet shouting,
  Shocked, in his mid-career.

Right on the Roman shield and sword 145
  Did spear of the Rhine maids run;
But the shield shifted never,
The sword rang down to sever,
The great Rhine sang for ever,
  And the songs of Elf were done.

And a great thunder of Christian men 151
  Went up against the sky,
Saying, "God hath broken the evil spear
  Ere the good man's blood was dry."

"Spears at the charge!" yelled Mark amain.   155
    "Death on the gods of death!
Over the thrones of doom and blood
Goeth God that is a craftsman good,
And gold and iron, earth and wood,
    Loveth and laboureth.

"The fruits leap up in all your farms,   161
    The lamps in each abode;
God of all good things done on earth,
All wheels or webs of any worth,
The God that makes the roof, Gurth,
    The God that makes the road.

"The God that heweth kings in oak   167
    Writeth songs on vellum,
God of gold and flaming glass,
Confregit potentias
Acrcuum, scutum, Gorlias,
    Gladium et bellum."

Steel and lightning broke about him,   173
    Battle-bays and palm,
All the sea-kings swayed among
Woods of the Wessex arms upflung,
The trumpet of the Roman tongue,
    The thunder of the psalm.

And midmost of that rolling field   179
    Ran Ogier ragingly,
Lashing at Mark, who turned his blow,

And brake the helm about his brow,
   And broke him to his knee.

Then Ogier heaved over his head 184
   His huge round shield of proof;
But Mark set one foot on the shield,
One on some sundered rock upheeled,
And towered above the tossing field,
   A statue on a roof.

Dealing far blows about the fight, 190
   Like thunder-bolts a-roam,
Like birds about the battle-field,
While Ogier writhed under his shield
   Like a tortoise in his dome.

But hate in the buried Ogier 195
   Was strong as pain in hell,
With bare brute hand from the inside
He burst the shield of brass and hide,
And a death-stroke to the Roman's side
   Sent suddenly and well.

Then the great statue on the shield 201
   Looked his last look around
With level and imperial eye;
And Mark, the man from Italy,
Fell in the sea of agony,
   And died without a sound.

And Ogier, leaping up alive,
  Hurled his huge shield away
Flying, as when a juggler flings
  A whizzing plate in play.

And held two arms up rigidly,
  And roared to all the Danes:
"Fallen is Rome, yea, fallen
  The city of the plains!

"Shall no man born remember,
  That breaketh wood or weald,
How long she stood on the roof of the world
  As he stood on my shield.

"The new wild world forgetteth her
  As foam fades on the sea,
How long she stood with her foot on Man
  As he with his foot on me.

"No more shall the brown men of the south
  Move like the ants in lines,
To quiet men with olives
  Or madden men with vines.

"No more shall the white towns of the south,
  Where Tiber and Nilus run,
Sitting around a secret sea
  Worship a secret sun.

"The blind gods roar for Rome fallen,
  And forum and garland gone,

G. K. Chesterton's Early Poetry

For the ice of the north is broken,
  And the sea of the north comes on.

"The blind gods roar and rave and dream   235
  Of all cities under the sea,
For the heart of the north is broken,
  And the blood of the north is free.

"Down from the dome of the world we come,   239
  Rivers on rivers down,
Under us swirl the sects and hordes
  And the high dooms we drown.

"Down from the dome of the world and down,   243
  Struck flying as a skiff
On a river in spate is spun and swirled
Until we come to the end of the world
  That breaks short, like a cliff.

"And when we come to the end of the world   248
  For me, I count it fit
To take the leap like a good river,
  Shot shrieking over it.

"But whatso hap at the end of the world,   252
  Where Nothing is struck and sounds,
It is not, by Thor, these monkish men
  These humbled Wessex hounds—

"Not this pale line of Christian hinds,   256
  This one white string of men,
Shall keep us back from the end of the world,

And the things that happen then.

"It is not Alfred's dwarfish sword, 260
   Nor Egbert's pigmy crown,
Shall stay us now that descend in thunder,
Rending the realms and the realms thereunder,
   Down through the world and down."

There was that in the wild men back of him, 265
   There was that in his own wild song,
A dizzy throbbing, a drunkard smoke,
That dazed to death all Wessex folk,
   And swept their spears along.

Vainly the sword of Colan 270
   And the axe of Alfred plied—
The Danes poured in like a brainless plague,
   And knew not when they died.

Prince Colan slew a score of them, 274
   And was stricken to his knee;
King Alfred slew a score and seven
   And was borne back on a tree.

Back to the black gate of the woods, 278
   Back up the single way,
Back by the place of the parting ways
   Christ's knights were whirled away.

And when they came to the parting ways 282
   Doom's heaviest hammer fell,
For the King was beaten, blind, at bay,

Down the right lane with his array,
But Colan swept the other way,
  Where he smote great strokes and fell.

The thorn-woods over Ethandune 288
  Stand sharp and thick as spears,
  By night and furze and forest-harms
  Far sundered were the friends in arms;
  The loud lost blows, the last alarms,
  Came not to Alfred's ears.

The thorn-woods over Ethandune 294
  Stand stiff as spikes in mail;
As to the Haut King came at morn
Dead Roland on a doubtful horn,
Seemed unto Alfred lightly borne
  The last cry of the Gael.

Book VII
Ethandune: The Last Charge

Away in the waste of White Horse Down
   An idle child alone
Played some small game through hours that pass,
And patiently would pluck the grass,
   Patiently push the stone.

On the lean, green edge for ever,   *6*
   Where the blank chalk touched the turf,
The child played on, alone, divine,
As a child plays on the last line
   That sunders sand and surf.

For he dwelleth in high divisions   *11*
   Too simple to understand,
Seeing on what morn of mystery
The Uncreated rent the sea
   With roarings, from the land.

Through the long infant hours like days   *16*
   He built one tower in vain—
Piled up small stones to make a town,
And evermore the stones fell down,
   And he piled them up again.

And crimson kings on battle-towers,   *21*
   And saints on Gothic spires,
And hermits on their peaks of snow,
   And heroes on their pyres,

       G. K. Chesterton's Early Poetry

And patriots riding royally,   25
  That rush the rocking town,
Stretch hands, and hunger and aspire,
Seeking to mount where high and higher,
The child whom Time can never tire,
  Sings over White Horse Down.

And this was the might of Alfred,   31
  At the ending of the way;
That of such smiters, wise or wild,
He was least distant from the child,
  Piling the stones all day.

For Eldred fought like a frank hunter   36
  That killeth and goeth home;
And Mark had fought because all arms
  Rang like the name of Rome.

And Colan fought with a double mind,   40
  Moody and madly gay;
But Alfred fought as gravely
  As a good child at play.

He saw wheels break and work run back   44
  And all things as they were;
And his heart was orbed like victory
  And simple like despair.

Therefore is Mark forgotten,   48
  That was wise with his tongue and brave;
And the cairn over Colan crumbled,

And the cross on Eldred's grave.

Their great souls went on a wind away, 52
   And they have not tale or tomb;
And Alfred born in Wantage
   Rules England till the doom.

Because in the forest of all fears 56
   Like a strange fresh gust from sea,
Struck him that ancient innocence
   That is more than mastery.

And as a child whose bricks fall down 60
   Re-piles them o'er and o'er,
Came ruin and the rain that burns,
Returning as a wheel returns,
And crouching in the furze and ferns
   He began his life once more.

He took his ivory horn unslung 66
   And smiled, but not in scorn:
"Endeth the Battle of Ethandune
   With the blowing of a horn."

On a dark horse at the double way 70
   He saw great Guthrum ride,
Heard roar of brass and ring of steel,
The laughter and the trumpet peal,
   The pagan in his pride.

And Ogier's red and hated head 75
   Moved in some talk or task;

But the men seemed scattered in the brier,
And some of them had lit a fire,
  And one had broached a cask.

And waggons one or two stood up,   80
  Like tall ships in sight,
As if an outpost were encamped
  At the cloven ways for night.

And joyous of the sudden stay   84
  Of Alfred's routed few,
Sat one upon a stone to sigh,
And some slipped up the road to fly,
Till Alfred in the fern hard by
  Set horn to mouth and blew.

And they all abode like statues—   90
  One sitting on the stone,
One half-way through the thorn hedge tall,
One with a leg across a wall,
And one looked backwards, very small,
  Far up the road, alone.

Grey twilight and a yellow star   96
  Hung over thorn and hill;
Two spears and a cloven war-shield lay
Loose on the road as cast away,
The horn died faint in the forest grey,
  And the fleeing men stood still.

"Brothers at arms," said Alfred,   *102*
　"On this side lies the foe;
Are slavery and starvation flowers,
　That you should pluck them so?

"For whether is it better   *106*
　To be prodded with Danish poles,
Having hewn a chamber in a ditch,
And hounded like a howling witch,
　Or smoked to death in holes?

"Or that before the red cock crow   *111*
　All we, a thousand strong,
Go down the dark road to God's house,
　Singing a Wessex song?

"To sweat a slave to a race of slaves,   *115*
　To drink up infamy?
No, brothers, by your leave, I think
Death is a better ale to drink,
And by all the stars of Christ that sink,
　The Danes shall drink with me.

"To grow old cowed in a conquered land,   *121*
　With the sun itself discrowned,
To see trees crouch and cattle slink—
Death is a better ale to drink,
And by high Death on the fell brink
　That flagon shall go round.

"Though dead are all the paladins   127
    Whom glory had in ken,
Though all your thunder-sworded thanes
With proud hearts died among the Danes,
While a man remains, great war remains:
    Now is a war of men.

"The men that tear the furrows,   133
    The men that fell the trees,
When all their lords be lost and dead
The bondsmen of the earth shall tread
    The tyrants of the seas.

"The wheel of the roaring stillness   138
    Of all labours under the sun,
Speed the wild work as well at least
    As the whole world's work is done.

"Let Hildred hack the shield-wall   142
    Clean as he hacks the hedge;
Let Gurth the fowler stand as cool
    As he stands on the chasm's edge;

"Let Gorlias ride the sea-kings   146
    As Gorlias rides the sea,
Then let all hell and Denmark drive,
Yelling to all its fiends alive,
    And not a rag care we."

When Alfred's word was ended   151
    Stood firm that feeble line,

Each in his place with club or spear,
And fury deeper than deep fear,
   And smiles as sour as brine.

And the King held up the horn and said, 156
   "See ye my father's horn,
That Egbert blew in his empery,
Once, when he rode out commonly,
Twice when he rode for venery,
   And thrice on the battle-morn.

"But heavier fates have fallen 162
   The horn of the Wessex kings,
And I blew once, the riding sign,
To call you to the fighting line
   And glory and all good things.

"And now two blasts, the hunting sign, 167
   Because we turn to bay;
But I will not blow the three blasts,
   Till we be lost or they.

"And now I blow the hunting sign, 171
   Charge some by rule and rod;
But when I blow the battle sign,
   Charge all and go to God."

Wild stared the Danes at the double ways 175
   Where they loitered, all at large,
As that dark line for the last time
   Doubled the knee to charge—

And caught their weapons clumsily, 179
   And marvelled how and why—
In such degree, by rule and rod,
The people of the peace of God
   Went roaring down to die.

And when the last arrow 184
   Was fitted and was flown,
When the broken shield hung on the breast,
And the hopeless lance was laid in rest,
   And the hopeless horn blown,

The King looked up, and what he saw 189
   Was a great light like death,
For Our Lady stood on the standards rent,
As lonely and as innocent
As when between white walls she went
   And the lilies of Nazareth.

One instant in a still light 195
   He saw Our Lady then,
Her dress was soft as western sky,
And she was a queen most womanly—
   But she was a queen of men.

Over the iron forest 200
   He saw Our Lady stand,
Her eyes were sad withouten art,
And seven swords were in her heart—
   But one was in her hand.

Then the last charge went blindly,   205
    And all too lost for fear:
The Danes closed round, a roaring ring,
And twenty clubs rose o'er the King,
Four Danes hewed at him, halloing,
And Ogier of the Stone and Sling
    Drove at him with a spear.

But the Danes were wild with laughter,   212
    And the great spear swung wide,
The point stuck to a straggling tree,
And either host cried suddenly,
    As Alfred leapt aside.

Short time had shaggy Ogier   217
    To pull his lance in line—
He knew King Alfred's axe on high,
    He heard it rushing through the sky,

He cowered beneath it with a cry—   221
    It split him to the spine:
And Alfred sprang over him dead,
    And blew the battle sign.

Then bursting all and blasting   225
    Came Christendom like death,
Kicked of such catapults of will,
The staves shiver, the barrels spill,
The waggons waver and crash and kill
    The waggoners beneath.

Barriers go backwards, banners rend,
  Great shields groan like a gong—
Horses like horns of nightmare
  Neigh horribly and long.

Horses ramp high and rock and boil
  And break their golden reins,
And slide on carnage clamorously,
Down where the bitter blood doth lie,
Where Ogier went on foot to die,
  In the old way of the Danes.

"The high tide!" King Alfred cried.
  "The high tide and the turn!
As a tide turns on the tall grey seas,
See how they waver in the trees,
How stray their spears, how knock their knees,
  How wild their watchfires burn!

"The Mother of God goes over them,
  Walking on wind and flame,
And the storm-cloud drifts from city and dale,
And the White Horse stamps in the White Horse
    Vale,
And we all shall yet drink Christian ale
  In the village of our name.

"The Mother of God goes over them,
  On dreadful cherubs borne;
And the psalm is roaring above the rune,
And the Cross goes over the sun and moon,

Endeth the battle of Ethandune
  With the blowing of a horn."

For back indeed disorderly   259
  The Danes went clamouring,
Too worn to take anew the tale,
Or dazed with insolence and ale,
Or stunned of heaven, or stricken pale
  Before the face of the King.

For dire was Alfred in his hour   265
  The pale scribe witnesseth,
More mighty in defeat was he
Than all men else in victory,
And behind, his men came murderously,
  Dry-throated, drinking death.

And Edgar of the Golden Ship   271
  He slew with his own hand,
Took Ludwig from his lady's bower,
And smote down Harmar in his hour,
And vain and lonely stood the tower—
  The tower in Guelderland.

And Torr out of his tiny boat,   277
  Whose eyes beheld the Nile,
Wulf with his war-cry on his lips,
And Harco born in the eclipse,
Who blocked the Seine with battleships
  Round Paris on the Isle.

And Hacon of the Harvest-Song,
   And Dirck from the Elbe he slew,
And Cnut that melted Durham bell
And Fulk and fiery Oscar fell,
And Goderic and Sigael,
   And Uriel of the Yew.

283

And highest sang the slaughter,
   And fastest fell the slain,
When from the wood-road's blackening throat
A crowning and crashing wonder smote
   The rear-guard of the Dane.

289

For the dregs of Colan's company—
   Lost down the other road—
Had gathered and grown and heard the din,
And with wild yells came pouring in,
Naked as their old British kin,
   And bright with blood for woad.

294

And bare and bloody and aloft
   They bore before their band
The body of the mighty lord,
Colan of Caerleon and its horde,
That bore King Alfred's battle-sword
   Broken in his left hand.

300

And a strange music went with him,
   Loud and yet strangely far;
The wild pipes of the western land,
Too keen for the ear to understand,

306

Sang high and deathly on each hand
  When the dead man went to war.

Blocked between ghost and buccaneer,   312
  Brave men have dropped and died;
And the wild sea-lords well might quail
As the ghastly war-pipes of the Gael
Called to the horns of White Horse Vale,
  And all the horns replied.

And Hildred the poor hedger   318
  Cut down four captains dead,
And Halmar laid three others low,
And the great earls wavered to and fro
  For the living and the dead.

And Gorlias grasped the great flag,   323
  The Raven of Odin, torn;
And the eyes of Guthrum altered,
  For the first time since morn.

As a turn of the wheel of tempest   327
  Tilts up the whole sky tall,
And cliffs of wan cloud luminous
Lean out like great walls over us,
  As if the heavens might fall.

As such a tall and tilted sky   332
  Sends certain snow or light,
So did the eyes of Guthrum change,
And the turn was more certain and more strange

Than a thousand men in flight.

For not till the floor of the skies is split,   337
  And hell-fire shines through the sea,
Or the stars look up through the rent earth's knees,
Cometh such rending of certainties,
As when one wise man truly sees
  What is more wise than he.

He set his horse in the battle-breech   343
  Even Guthrum of the Dane,
And as ever had fallen fell his brand,
A falling tower o'er many a land,
But Gurth the fowler laid one hand
  Upon this bridle rein.

King Guthrum was a great lord,   349
  And higher than his gods—
He put the popes to laughter,
  He chid the saints with rods,

He took this hollow world of ours   353
  For a cup to hold his wine;
In the parting of the woodways
  There came to him a sign.

In Wessex in the forest,   357
  In the breaking of the spears,
We set a sign on Guthrum
  To blaze a thousand years.

Where the high saddles jostle 361
    And the horse-tails toss,
There rose to the birds flying
A roar of dead and dying;
In deafness and strong crying
    We signed him with the cross.

Far out to the winding river 367
    The blood ran down for days,
When we put the cross on Guthrum
    In the parting of the ways.

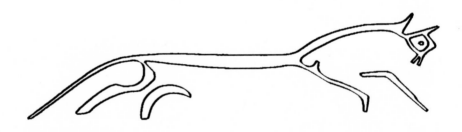

Book VIII
The Scouring of the Horse

In the years of the peace of Wessex,
  When the good King sat at home;
Years following on that bloody boon
When she that stands above the moon
Stood above death at Ethandune
  And saw his kingdom come—

When the pagan people of the sea   7
  Fled to their palisades,
Nailed there with javelins to cling
And wonder smote the pirate king,
And brought him to his christening
  And the end of all his raids.

(For not till the night's blue slate is wiped   13
  Of its last star utterly,
And fierce new signs writ there to read,
Shall eyes with such amazement heed,
As when a great man knows indeed
  A greater thing than he.)

And there came to his chrism-loosing   19
  Lords of all lands afar,
And a line was drawn north-westerly
That set King Egbert's empire free,
Giving all lands by the northern sea
  To the sons of the northern star.

In the days of the rest of Alfred,   25
    When all these things were done,
And Wessex lay in a patch of peace,
    Like a dog in a patch of sun—

The King sat in his orchard,   29
    Among apples green and red,
With the little book in his bosom
    And the sunshine on his head.

And he gathered the songs of simple men   33
    That swing with helm and hod,
And the alms he gave as a Christian
Like a river alive with fishes ran;
And he made gifts to a beggar man
    As to a wandering god.

And he gat good laws of the ancient kings,   39
    Like treasure out of the tombs;
And many a thief in thorny nook,
Or noble in sea-stained turret shook,
For the opening of his iron book,
    And the gathering of the dooms.

Then men would come from the ends of the earth,   45
    Whom the King sat welcoming,
And men would go to the ends of the earth
    Because of the word of the King.

For folk came in to Alfred's face   49
    Whose javelins had been hurled

On monsters that make boil the sea,
Crakens and coils of mystery.
Or thrust in ancient snows that be
  The white hair of the world.

And some had knocked at the northern gates   55
  Of the ultimate icy floor,
Where the fish freeze and the foam turns black,
And the wide world narrows to a track,
And the other sea at the world's back
  Cries through a closed door.

And men went forth from Alfred's face,   61
  Even great gift-bearing lords,
Not to Rome only, but more bold,
Out to the high hot courts of old,
Of negroes clad in cloth of gold,
  Silence, and crooked swords,

Scrawled screens and secret gardens   67
  And insect-laden skies—
Where fiery plains stretch on and on
To the purple country of Prester John
  And the walls of Paradise.

And he knew the might of the Terre Majeure,   72
  Where kings began to reign;
Where in a night-rout, without name,
Of gloomy Goths and Gauls there came
White, above candles all aflame,
  Like a vision, Charlemagne.

The Ballad of the White Horse

And men, seeing such embassies, 78
    Spake with the King and said:
"The steel that sang so sweet a tune
On Ashdown and on Ethandune,
Why hangs it scabbarded so soon,
    All heavily like lead?

"Why dwell the Danes in North England, 84
    And up to the river ride?
Three more such marches like thine own
Would end them; and the Pict should own
Our sway; and our feet climb the throne
    In the mountains of Strathclyde."

And Alfred in the orchard, 90
    Among apples green and red,
With the little book in his bosom,
    Looked at green leaves and said:

"When all philosophies shall fail, 94
    This word alone shall fit;
That a sage feels too small for life,
    And a fool too large for it.

"Asia and all imperial plains 98
    Are too little for a fool;
But for one man whose eyes can see
The little island of Athelney
    Is too large a land to rule.

"Haply it had been better   103
   When I built my fortress there,
Out in the reedy waters wide,
I had stood on my mud wall and cried:
'Take England all, from tide to tide—
   Be Athelney my share.'

"Those madmen of the throne-scramble—   109
   Oppressors and oppressed—
Had lined the banks by Athelney,
And waved and wailed unceasingly,
Where the river turned to the broad sea,
   By an island of the blest.

"An island like a little book   115
   Full of a hundred tales,
Like the gilt page the good monks pen,
That is all smaller than a wren,
Yet hath high towns, meteors, and men,
   And suns and spouting whales;

"A land having a light on it   121
   In the river dark and fast,
An isle with utter clearness lit,
Because a saint had stood in it;
Where flowers are flowers indeed and fit,
   And trees are trees at last.

"So were the island of a saint;   127
   But I am a common king,
And I will make my fences tough

From Wantage Town to Plymouth Bluff,
Because I am not wise enough
   To rule so small a thing."

And it fell in the days of Alfred,   133
   In the days of his repose,
That as old customs in his sight
Were a straight road and a steady light,
He bade them keep the White Horse white
   As the first plume of the snows.

And right to the red torchlight,   139
   From the trouble of morning grey,
They stripped the White Horse of the grass
   As they strip it to this day.

And under the red torchlight   143
   He went dreaming as though dull,
Of his old companions slain like kings,
And the rich irrevocable things
Of a heart that hath not openings,
   But is shut fast, being full.

And the torchlight touched the pale hair   149
   Where silver clouded gold,
And the frame of his face was made of cords,
And a young lord turned among the lords
   And said: "The King is old."

And even as he said it   154
   A post ran in amain,

Crying: "Arm, Lord King, the hamlets arm,
In the horror and the shade of harm,
They have burnt Brand of Aynger's farm—
  The Danes are come again!

"Danes drive the white East Angles   160
  In six fights on the plains,
Danes waste the world about the Thames,
  Danes to the eastward—Danes!"

And as he stumbled on one knee,   164
  The thanes broke out in ire,
Crying: "Ill the watchmen watch, and ill
  The sheriffs keep the shire."

But the young earl said: "Ill the saints,   168
  The saints of England, guard
The land wherein we pledge them gold;
The dykes decay, the King grows old,
  And surely this is hard,

"That we be never quit of them;   173
  That when his head is hoar
He cannot say to them he smote,
And spared with a hand hard at the throat,
  'Go, and return no more.'"

Then Alfred smiled. And the smile of him   178
  Was like the sun for power.
But he only pointed: bade them heed
Those peasants of the Berkshire breed,

Who plucked the old Horse of the weed
　　As they pluck it to this hour.

"Will ye part with the weeds for ever?　　184
　　Or show daisies to the door?
Or will you bid the bold grass
　　Go, and return no more?

"So ceaseless and so secret　　188
　　Thrive terror and theft set free;
Treason and shame shall come to pass
While one weed flowers in a morass;
And like the stillness of stiff grass
　　The stillness of tyranny.

"Over our white souls also　　194
　　Wild heresies and high
Wave prouder than the plumes of grass,
　　And sadder than their sigh.

"And I go riding against the raid,　　198
　　And ye know not where I am;
But ye shall know in a day or year,
When one green star of grass grows here;
Chaos has charged you, charger and spear,
　　Battle-axe and battering-ram.

"And though skies alter and empires melt,　　204
　　This word shall still be true:
If we would have the horse of old,
　　Scour ye the horse anew.

"One time I followed a dancing star   *208*
   That seemed to sing and nod,
And ring upon earth all evil's knell;
But now I wot if ye scour not well
Red rust shall grow on God's great bell
   And grass in the streets of God."

Ceased Alfred; and above his head   *214*
   The grand green domes, the Downs,
Showed the first legions of the press,
Marching in haste and bitterness
   For Christ's sake and the crown's.

Beyond the cavern of Colan,   *219*
   Past Eldred's by the sea,
Rose men that owned King Alfred's rod,
From the windy wastes of Exe untrod,
Or where the thorn of the grave of God
   Burns over Glastonbury.

Far northward and far westward   *225*
   The distant tribes drew nigh,
Plains beyond plains, fell beyond fell,
That a man at sunset sees so well,
And the tiny coloured towns that dwell
   In the corners of the sky.

But dark and thick as thronged the host,   *231*
   With drum and torch and blade,
The still-eyed King sat pondering,
As one that watches a live thing,

The scoured chalk; and he said,

"Though I give this land to Our Lady,   236
    That helped me in Athelney,
Though lordlier trees and lustier sod
And happier hills hath no flesh trod
Than the garden of the Mother of God
    Between Thames side and the sea,

"I know that weeds shall grow in it   242
    Faster than men can burn;
And though they scatter now and go,
In some far century, sad and slow,
I have a vision, and I know
    The heathen shall return.

"They shall not come with warships,   248
    They shall not waste with brands,
But books be all their eating,
    And ink be on their hands.

"Not with the humour of hunters   252
    Or savage skill in war,
But ordering all things with dead words,
Strings shall they make of beasts and birds,
    And wheels of wind and star.

"They shall come mild as monkish clerks,   257
    With many a scroll and pen;
And backward shall ye turn and gaze,
Desiring one of Alfred's days,

When pagans still were men.

"The dear sun dwarfed of dreadful suns, 262
  Like fiercer flowers on stalk,
Earth lost and little like a pea
In high heaven's towering forestry,
—These be the small weeds ye shall see
  Crawl, covering the chalk.

"But though they bridge St. Mary's sea, 268
  Or steal St. Michael's wing—
Though they rear marvels over us,
  Greater than great Vergilius
  Wrought for the Roman king;

"By this sign you shall know them, 273
  The breaking of the sword,
And man no more a free knight,
  That loves or hates his lord.

"Yea, this shall be the sign of them, 277
  The sign of the dying fire;
And Man made like a half-wit,
  That knows not of his sire.

"What though they come with scroll and pen, 281
  And grave as a shaven clerk,
By this sign you shall know them,
  That they ruin and make dark;

"By all men bond to Nothing, 285
  Being slaves without a lord,

By one blind idiot world obeyed,
  Too blind to be abhorred;

"By terror and the cruel tales   *289*
  Of curse in bone and kin,
By weird and weakness winning,
Accursed from the beginning,
By detail of the sinning,
  And denial of the sin;

"By thought a crawling ruin,   *295*
  By life a leaping mire,
By a broken heart in the breast of the world,
  And the end of the world's desire;

"By God and man dishonoured,   *299*
  By death and life made vain,
Know ye the old barbarian,
  The barbarian come again—

"When is great talk of trend and tide,   *303*
  And wisdom and destiny,
Hail that undying heathen
  That is sadder than the sea.

"In what wise men shall smite him,   *307*
  Or the Cross stand up again,
Or charity or chivalry,
My vision saith not; and I see
No more; but now ride doubtfully
  To the battle of the plain."

And the grass-edge of the great down 313
  Was cut clean as a lawn,
While the levies thronged from near and far,
From the warm woods of the western star,
And the King went out to his last war
  On a tall grey horse at dawn.

And news of his far-off fighting 319
  Came slowly and brokenly
From the land of the East Saxons,
  From the sunrise and the sea.

From the plains of the white sunrise, 323
  And sad St. Edmund's crown,
Where the pools of Essex pale and gleam
  Out beyond London Town—

In mighty and doubtful fragments, 327
  Like faint or fabled wars,
Climbed the old hills of his renown,
Where the bald brow of White Horse Down
  Is close to the cold stars.

But away in the eastern places 332
  The wind of death walked high,
And a raid was driven athwart the raid,
The sky reddened and the smoke swayed,
  And the tall grey horse went by.

The gates of the great river 337
  Were breached as with a barge,

The walls sank crowded, say the scribes,
And high towers populous with tribes
   Seemed leaning from the charge.

Smoke like rebellious heavens rolled 342
   Curled over coloured flames,
Mirrored in monstrous purple dreams
   In the mighty pools of Thames.

Loud was the war on London wall, 346
   And loud in London gates,
And loud the sea-kings in the cloud
Broke through their dreaming gods, and loud
   Cried on their dreadful Fates.

And all the while on White Horse Hill 351
   The horse lay long and wan,
The turf crawled and the fungus crept,
And the little sorrel, while all men slept,
   Unwrought the work of man.

With velvet finger, velvet foot, 356
   The fierce soft mosses then
Crept on the large white commonweal
All folk had striven to strip and peel,
And the grass, like a great green witch's wheel,
   Unwound the toils of men.

And clover and silent thistle throve, 362
   And buds burst silently,
With little care for the Thames Valley

Or what things there might be—

That away on the widening river,
  In the eastern plains for crown
Stood up in the pale purple sky
One turret of smoke like ivory;
And the smoke changed and the wind went by,
  And the King took London Town.

Printed in the United Kingdom
by Lightning Source UK Ltd.
109041UKS00001B/306